I0421926

CREATIVITY

A HANDBOOK FOR

VISUAL ARTISTS

CREATIVITY
A HANDBOOK FOR
VISUAL ARTISTS

JONATHAN SANSOM

Imagework Publishing
Cambridge
England

First published 2012
by Imagework Publishing
1 Chelmer Way, Ely, Cambs, CB6 2WS
England, UK

© Jonathan Sansom 2012
www.jonathansansom.net

Illustrations by Lucy Sansom

All rights reserved. No part of this book may be reprinted or
reproduced or utilised in any form or by any electronic, mechanical, or
by other means, now known or hereafter invented, including
photocopying or recording, or in any other information storage or
retrieval system, without permission in writing from the publishers.

British Library Cataloguing in Publishing Data
A catalogue record for this book is available from the British Library

ISBN: 978-0-9571228-0-2

Typeset in Palatino Linotype

Printed and distributed by Lightning Source UK Ltd.

*with thanks to all who
have supported this project,
especially my family*

Contents

Foreword

This book is a discussion about the nature of creativity in the visual arts. I have called it a 'handbook' as it includes both the examination of key ideas and themes as well as suggestions of practical strategies to enhance and develop visual creativity.

The famous Haynes' manuals for cars are based on an expert taking a vehicle apart, carrying out maintenance and repairs and photographing each stage; novices can see the processes and structure revealed so clearly that an old Renault 5, for example, has no mystery and any job can be tackled with confidence as long as you have a reasonable set of tools. Just as the car handbook is divided up into related sections, such as transmission and electrical systems, I have also attempted to make some useful divisions to reveal something of the constituent 'parts' of visual creativity. Of course this analogy is not perfect, not least since creativity is a difficult to pin down human quality, rather than a physical object; nevertheless I hope I can show that it is quite possible to identify some of the key aspects of creativity and to discover something of the relationships they reveal. I don't consider myself to be an expert; however I have had an interest in this area which spans thirty years. My own journey into visual creativity has taken many twists and turns and so informs much of the content of this book. My initial training was as a painter at

Wimbledon School of Art in the 1980s. Here I immersed myself in my subject and remember feeling when I left that I could not have had a better education as an artist. At this time I also started to explore ideas about the psychology of art and this was a significant start to my particular journey.

After leaving art college I worked for a few years in the mental health sector and trained as a psychodynamic counsellor; this continued to develop my thinking on change and creativity. Later I moved to book and publicity design, taking part in the desktop publishing revolution in the early 1990s. This was a long way from fine art and mental health, but I found gaining commercial experience of visual design rewarding as it demanded a quite different approach.

In 1993 I returned to education to study for a postgraduate degree in Art and Psychotherapy; at the same time I also started to teach art part-time in a secondary school. These activities complemented each other well as I was able to combine research into the nature of the imagination with the very pragmatic challenges of learning to teach in an 11-18 secondary school.

At present I lead an art and design department in a sixth form college and have the privilege of working with many students who are making their first decisions about training in the visual arts. We have young fine artists, graphic and product designers, architects, film makers and fashion designers studying with us. These are students for whom the development of their own imagination and creativity is a vital cornerstone on which to build as they move on to take up specialist study in the arts.

The practical strategies I discuss have largely arisen from my own approach to teaching. They act as a foil to the main ideas and illustrate how it is always possible to take action to explore and develop work in creative ways. These suggestions are not specific to any particular discipline and most may be equally suitable for designers and architects as much as for painters or sculptors. The practical ideas are targeted at the generative stage of creative work where new possibilities are opened out and, as the reader will discover, they tackle this in many different ways.

Creating my own work remains an important and fascinating activity, as it does for many who teach art and design. To explore the world imaginatively through making, remains the true testing ground for the ideas of which I write here. I hope that what is discussed is of interest and useful for those who study the visual arts, and for whom the development of creativity is also a real and challenging part of their experience.

Jonathan Sansom
January 2012

PART I

FIRST PRINCIPLES

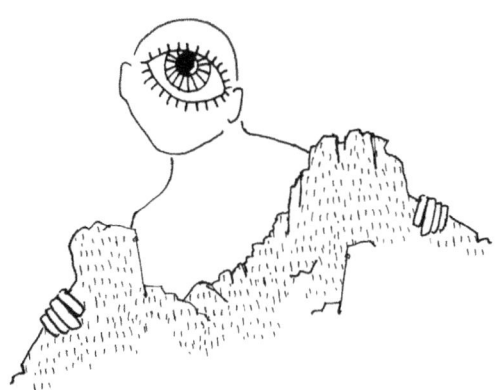

IMAGES AT THE BEGINNING

What is the earliest significant memory you have of art making?
How far back can you go? Think of the moment when you first
realised that making art held something special for you.

I think I must have been about six or seven years old when my
parents said that they planned to give me a big book called an
'encyclopaedia'. I remember clearly what I assumed the book
would be like; the biggest book I had was a sugar paper scrap-
book which was probably about A3 size. I had a vision of a giant
sugar paper book arriving, maybe as big as a table.

When it arrived I remember my surprise when I saw that it
was actually not a giant stapled paperback. In fact it fitted in a
normal book shelf since its size was due to the number of pages
rather than the page dimensions.

I consider this to be probably my earliest significant art
memory as I still vividly remember four key images that were
in the book. The encyclopaedia itself was beautifully produced,
printed on fine glossy white paper with a generous number of
high quality colour reproductions. It was the images in the book
which drew me in; I remember that I could read bits of it, but the
fascination with the pictures was the main thing.

I remember a picture of an X-ray of a fractured bone and three paintings and absolutely nothing else. Yet these images, even now as I write, getting on for forty years later, remain vivid. I know the paintings well now, yet I also clearly remember seeing them in the book then.

Each of the reproductions was set within the text and was no more than about eight centimetres in height, yet the quality was such that the detail and colour were sharp and clear.

The first image was the Death of Marat by Jacques-Louis David (1793). The entry in the book may have been either under 'David' or perhaps 'French Revolution', I recall that I understood that the man had been killed whilst having a bath, and that this was an image from history depicting a real event. I was struck by the strangeness of the image as well as the high drama. Why was the man bathing with an arrangement of sheets and blankets covering the bath?

Writing in the bath also seemed odd; I had no idea what he was writing, though I could see it added to the drama and to the depiction of an actual event.

The stark puncture wound made by the knife, just below Marat's collar bone, appeared to gape slightly and although there was little blood on his chest there was some on the sheet below, and just under his outstretched arm it appeared that the almost over-filled bath had itself been turned blood red. The weapon discarded on the floor was a simple domestic bone handled knife. I had seen such knives amongst the ancient cutlery brought out when my parents took me to tea at my great aunts' house. Cora and Nina were my mother's aunts; both had lost sweethearts in the First World War, neither had married, and in the early 1970s they still lived in the family home which their father, a carpenter, had helped to build in the early 20th Century.

Visiting this house as a small child was a little like stepping back in time, in my imagination I made a link between the small bone handled murder weapon and my own connections to history and the past. Cora and Nina did not exactly belong to the world of the French Revolution but I suspect some of their cutlery may well have gone back that far.

I did not realise it at the time, but in many ways this small reproduction was affecting me in exactly the way that David intended his contemporary viewers to respond. This was a beautiful death not an ugly one; it was serene, dignified, theatrical and heroic. Marat looked beautiful and the way that his body rested suggested sleep more than death. The light falling on his arms and face, across the draped sheets and the turban style head covering was a handsome image, this was exaggerated by the brooding darkness of the plain upper half of the picture. At this impressionable age I had also seen Hollywood films about the Classical world on Saturday morning TV, perhaps Antony and Cleopatra, 300 Spartans or something similar. I remember that I drew pictures of Roman and Greek battles with stick men. With no knowledge of the French fashions of Neoclassicism at all, I could still pick up on the visual link between the play of light on the sheets and images of film stars in togas. It all looked like an ancient dignified world; I did not realise that this was a product of David's deliberate style and idealism, yet I certainly responded to it. In this way David's Marat crept into my imaginative world.

The second image I recall so vividly was Salvador Dali's Soft Construction with Boiled Beans (Premonition of Civil War) from 1936. It is easy to understand why. This is one of Dali's most monstrous and disturbing images; it presents a piled up construction of corpse parts, the head in a deathly grimace, a hand grasping at an engorged breast. The crude naked anatomy is reconfigured into a new impossible form and then given the illusion of immense scale, with the inclusion of a small grey-suited observer who appears to be studying the grotesque hand at the base of the image. For all its strangeness it appears every bit as real as the Marat; it occupies a convincing pictorial space, a barren landscape with a backdrop of dramatic white clouds against a rich blue sky beyond. It is no wonder it caught my attention, as it would any small child. It is utterly fascinating and fantastic, overtly repulsive and yet absolutely beautiful in its execution.

The brutal physicality and the disturbed sexual nature of the image has an impact on any viewer, perhaps even more so on a small child and it certainly struck me. I now understand that Dali was deliberately playing with dimensions of Freudian unconscious fantasy. I certainly don't recall if this was mentioned in the encyclopaedia entry, and even if it was it would have meant nothing, but perhaps the perverse theatricality had an impact at a purely intuitive level. It is an image that once seen sticks in the mind.

The third image I recall vividly and perhaps most strongly of the three was Odilon Redon's 'The Cyclops' (1914). I realise now with some curiosity that the title of the painting is itself a part of the word encyclopaedia, I don't recall whether I actually noticed this at the time. The significance of the image was fuelled by reading a childrens' text of Homer's Odyssey. I loved the epic tale; it was a gripping yarn, without a doubt, but I also

14

responded to it as a myth. I knew it was a story, but I also knew that at least parts of it depicted some kind of historical truth, but which bits, the Sirens, or even the Cyclops perhaps?

The book I had read had a series of small black and white illustrations at the top of each chapter-heading and some larger ones in the text. These were all drawn in the style of Hellenic vase decorations, very elegant, theatrical but almost as symbols of the drama rather than believable illustrations. It was left to my young imagination to create visions of the events as I read.

Seeing the Redon Cyclops in the encyclopaedia added a whole new dimension to this experience, for it was both familiar and yet completely unexpected. It certainly showed a giant with one eye in the centre of its forehead yet it was much more than an illustration. Redon depicts the monster as a gentle giant, almost childlike; the head is a disc ringed by hair, ears, the mouth smudged and indistinct, the single eye is at the centre and a soft almost pathetic gaze meets the viewer directly.

Beneath the Cyclops embedded in the rich vegetation of the island is Odysseus himself. Naked, his body is turned away from the centre and he sleeps. The sleeping hero and the monster are completely unaware of the presence of the other, yet the viewer sees both and their perilous proximity. It is an odd image since it presents a sense of peace and repose, the calm innocence of the giant, the vulnerable sleep of Odysseus and this is all set against the incredibly rich colours and textures of the landscape. It is like an image of paradise which has had the ancient drama poured into it and the terror, threat and danger of the scene has been transformed into a dreamlike idyll.

This third image made the biggest impact without a doubt. It connected with a familiar story but on a deeper level it also presented an image of an archaic dream world, a world which a young child is perhaps closer to than any adult. Sleep, dreaming, the developing conscious mind and growing knowledge of the world, frame the very early years of life when the entire world is a dream, mysterious, unconnected and emotionally charged with both anxiety and pleasure. I believe this image took me back to some of this experience and even now I think it still has the power to do this.

These three images, the David, Dali and Redon stand as an important beginning to my personal journey as an artist. To an extent this book is a continuation of this, as my focus is very much on how artists develop and grow their own creative experience and ability. The early memory of these images is a good place to start, since at a fundamental level creativity is about the articulation of formative moments. New experiences create an impact and then an artist responds by making a new object or image. This in turn provides a new type of experience for the artist and others, as ideas meld, synthesise and change.

I have called this introduction 'Images at the Beginning' since exploring visual creativity requires some thoughts about what actually constitues an image. The word itself can have a variety of meanings depending on context, so it is useful to outline an understanding of the particular role of images for artists and designers.

My experience of the pictures in the encyclopaedia still has a psychic presence even now some forty years later. I still have not seen the originals, though I have seen further reproductions many times. The David is in Belgium, the Dali in Philadelphia and the Redon in the Kröller Muller Museum in Holland. It is quite true that seeing actual art work can have a more profound effect than any reproduction. This is especially true for three dimensional works, installation or any work where an encounter with the physical material properties of the art is essential to the experience. However it would be wrong to confuse 'image' with the original art work. Image is a quality; it is how art presents itself to a viewer. I experienced the small reproductions as powerful images and indeed artists view images as a full and complex experience, which can take the viewer well beyond the initial act of looking. Pictures, sculptures or any form of visual art are never images in their own right; art only 'becomes' an image through interaction with the creators and viewers.

Image has long been held to be psychological, or at least something that is experienced, rather than existing separately somehow within the art we create. This is most clear when we realise that two people might have radically different experiences of the same art work; the 'image' experienced is different because of the difference in what the two viewers bring to the activity of looking. Image occurs in the experiencing not in the object.

The 20th century psychologist Carl Jung proposed that our entire experience is based on images and in his view 'image' is the fundamental quality of our lived experience. It is not an extra or an occasional experience; rather he described how images are more like a medium we move through as our very existence unfolds. Image is like water and we move through it rather like aquatic image creatures and, according to Jung, it is a defining aspect of our being. This makes sense when we think of how much our experience is shaped by 'image'. Politicians have images, as do desirable products and images also shape religious experience. The global entertainment industry manufactures images of celebrity, style, fashion and fame; and of course we have our own projected image that can take on guises and qualities according to the circumstances in which we find ourselves. Artists are creators of images; we conjure with the very stuff of this experience. No matter how humble a piece of art, we know that for the viewer it can, in a matter of a moment, blend into their psychic world, to move them, to create emotions, associations and thoughts and set their mind into the mood and context of the work. It can also affect, change and develop the experience of others. As artists we want no less; this is the work we set images to do.

These images have an independent life as they go into the world; and yet as we work, the images we create are also a part of us. As developing artists we become increasingly sensitive to images and their qualities.

The Jungian analyst and writer James Hillman describes how we might interact with an image in a range of ways using a dream as an example:

> When I am in a dream at night it is like a scene: and when I am pervaded by the dream during the day, it is like a mood.... An image perceived as a picture can tend to become optical and intellectual and distanced. It there, we here. But imagined as a scene, I can get into it; and when 'imaged' as a mood it gets into me.... When considered in this light, an image cannot be something only set before my eyeballs, or even before my mind's eye, since it is also something into which I enter and

by which I am embraced. Images hold us; we can be in the grip of an image.[1]

This is a powerful way of thinking about our own created images. We can imagine our art work as a dramatic scene and then imagine what has just happened, or what happens next. As a mood, what does it really feel like? If you could magically inhabit the art work, how exactly would you feel in that moment? If in the morning, the image you have created was your dream then what feeling comes with this moment as you awake from it?

These practical imaginative strategies can help move an image forward during production and also help to focus on the experiences which our artwork creates for ourselves, and other viewers.

Visual artists work with images because they have a specific power to communicate and engage viewers in a unique way. We all know the saying that a picture is worth a thousand words and this relationship to language is complex. When I was training to teach art I can remember being led to believe that we explored visual 'language' with our students and taught them visual 'literacy'. This type of talk was partly to act as a defence against cuts in the UK national art curriculum and to propose that art was as tough and as essential as English, Maths and Science. Without this special type of literacy young people would be unable to decipher the rich contemporary world of visual signs and media, and so would not take a productive and properly educated place in society.

---

1   Hillman, Further Notes on Images, p. 159.

19

I have sympathy with this view and it does make some sense. However this type of technical and instrumental view of learning may have degraded the engagement with the poetic content of visual art for many, including, one suspects, the teachers of art themselves. There is a risk of failure to engage with the primal quality of visual images and the reasons they can hold such power for us. Gerard Richter expresses this very clearly:

> 'Talk about painting: there's no point. By conveying a thing through the medium of language you change it. You construct qualities that can be said and you leave out the ones that can't be said but are always the most important.' [2]

This applies to any art which presents us with an image and is certainly not limited to only painting. Richter describes how images can provide an experience which is profoundly different from spoken language, and that it is naïve to think that we can analyse art to reveal content simply by talking about it.

Visual artists choose to create images often precisely because of the opportunity to work with this inarticulate and unspoken content. This is a world where images 'look right', really start to 'work'; the evaluation of success and anticipation of the next steps takes the artist into an internal world of intuition, complex emotions and judgements which are sometimes quite difficult to put into words. Often it is simply best and even necessary, for an artist just to keep quiet.

There is however another interesting way to consider how artists relate to images using language. It is abundantly clear that

---

2   Richter, The Daily Practice of Painting, p. 39.

when we visit exhibitions or if we are in the presence of artists, designers or other creative individuals, that conversation can become very rich and add to our experience of specific images. Are we really to take Richter at his word and warn people to keep quiet since they are missing the point of the work? Clearly something else is going on, but what?

Consider the experience of watching a really good TV programme about an artist or designer, presented by an excellent critic or indeed a fellow artist. We watch the flow of images, hear the stories and perhaps understand more about the context and the history of the work, as we listen to the presenter's thoughts about key images. If the experience is good and the presenter is imaginative and passionate about the work, we gain a stronger connection to the images. This is not limited to TV documentaries as it is a profound dimension of how we experience our relationship to images. It is not simply about language being used to 'explain' images; indeed this is precisely what Richter rightly objects to. Instead, language can be used to amplify and develop a relationship to images. The good presenter or teacher uses imaginative language, metaphors and analogies to enliven the experience of the images and in this way passion and energy increases our sense of connection and the experience becomes fuller. Hillman states that we do not speak about an image to seek to explain it or to find a hidden meaning, rather we should 'feed it with further images that increase its volume and depth and release its fecundity'.[3]

Viewed in this way it is clear that creativity for any visual artist should have an imaginative relationship to all images at

3   Hillman, A Blue Fire, p. 60.

the centre. This should underpin the work of an artist. We cannot simply be creative in the production of visual art without an imaginative attitude towards the images we encounter, since how we live with the images of others and indeed the images of the wider world we inhabit, is itself a creative act. It is this relationship to images which supplies the energy and the motivation for individual creativity and as Hillman says, this has the potential to increase the volume and depth of this experience and to release life itself.

All this talk of images and life runs the risk of sounding very worthy. Images have no inherent positive quality, of course, we live in a world where images are a forceful part of our experience at every level and can often have profoundly negative dimensions. Precisely because of the way in which images can connect with our emotional and imaginative experience, they also reflect much less positive aspects of our humanity.

At the furthest end of the spectrum images are used to stimulate hatred and intolerance and to support injustice of all kinds. This relationship between images and behaviour is complex yet evident in many areas. For example the global pornography industry is built on the manipulation of desire through imagery which in turn generates money. In the past, the church commissioned graphic images of torment in hell to teach populations the consequences of sin and so to instil moral behaviour. Within economic systems advertising seeks to steer behaviour primarily through images. Images in these contexts are never simple communications; they are loaded with associations, emotional content, desire and agendas of those who produce them. This image content is also sometimes wild and unpredictable; images have something of a life of their own. Advertising can for example miss the target audience, or even on occasions have the complete opposite effect of that which is intended.

Much of the discussion in this book needs to be understood against this cultural background and our 'life of images'. Artists and designers do not work in a vacuum; indeed visual artists are those who are often the most attuned to the image based culture which we inhabit.

Imagine that your work is suddenly viewed for the first time. Help this by taking it to a new location, out of the studio or workplace and away from the setting in which it may have become over familiar. Place the work at a distance and encounter it afresh, approach it slowly and look carefully at the image. For a moment try to do this without your usual artistic baggage, no clutter of concerns, no anxiety, no ambition or intentions. You are no longer the creator; it is there and you are here simple. What do you see? Reflect on this experience.

Work with a partner to identify a picture or object by an artist which one of you likes and the other dislikes, examine your reactions, discuss why you feel so differently about the same piece of art. You see the same sight but the experience of the image is very different. Why is this so? Unpack the specific nature of this experience.

What is the earliest memory you have of an image made by an artist? Why do you think you remember it? When exactly do you first remember seeing it? Try to get a copy of it for your journal, find out more about it and move it from memory into the present.

Test out how an image is functioning. Invite others to comment on the work, encourage them to speak without voicing your own opinion; in this way they can help you cut loose from the ideas in your mind which might be clouding what is actually being presented from the image to an audience. It is sometimes difficult to put yourself in the shoes of another, so let them keep their shoes on.

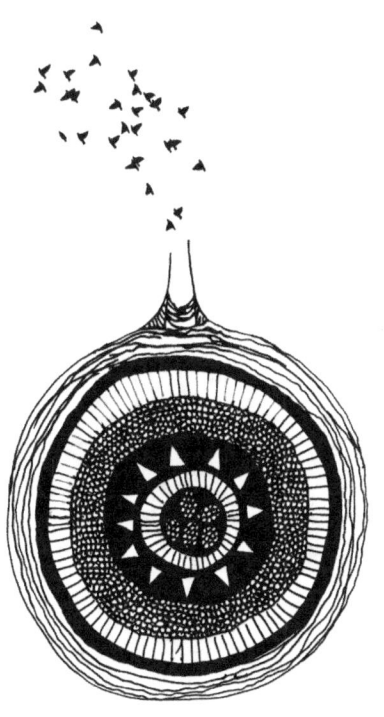

Transformation

Creativity is often thought of as a practical dimension of what it is to be human; it can be quite simply how we make things that are new.

We are all creative to greater or lesser degrees; this might be through making artwork, but equally it might be how we create relationships with others, or make a meal, or tend a garden. There are myriad opportunities for us to be creative and it is evident that the human world is a made world, a created world, full of things which are brought into being by a force of human ingenuity which for good or ill defines us all.

Some of our most distant ancestors painted beautiful images of animals and hunting on the walls of caves. These might have been made to bring the wildness and drama of nature into the home, perhaps to aid with story-telling, for mystic or poetic reasons, or for decorative pleasure; most likely it was for a combination of these things. Such images seem to indicate that the artistic creative urge is deeply rooted.

The American abstract expressionist painter, Barnett Newman, once stated that 'the first man was an artist'. He speculated that 'just as man's first speech was poetic before it became utilitarian, so man first built an idol of mud before he fashioned an axe'[4].

Newman's view is that the drive to create is not to master the world but to imagine it, to create forms and images which develop relationship and meaning and help us know in a full sense what the world is like. Our ancestor artists created images to share and reflect on experience, cave paintings are unlikely to have been simply maps of where the food was. The flair and style of the imagery suggest much more that they were made to display the spectacle of nature and the hunt for those who viewed them.

The ability to reflect on life through the invention of forms and images is an important human capacity and this is not limited solely to the arts. The great artist and teacher Joseph Beuys stated that 'if creativity relates to the transformation, change, and development of substance, then it can be applied to everything in the world and is no longer restricted to art...'[5] Beuys encourages to us to view creativity as democratic, ubiquitous and at the very centre of our relationship to the world, one which develops and changes our experience and also that of others. This applies as much to science and technology as it does to the arts.

Our creativity as a species may have a distant and mysterious beginning at which we can only guess, but there is a beginning to which we all have access and can more easily observe. This is the imaginative journey which we begin as small children.

---

4   Newman, The First Man Was an Artist
5   Beuys, from the film Transformer

In order to contribute to the world in a creative way there is much for a young person to learn and learning and creativity are bound together from birth. Picasso's famous quote that 'every child is an artist' refers to the innate ability we have from our very earliest years to play, to discover and to make. The roots of the visual arts explored through drawing, painting and making, often with humble materials, are an essential dimension to the early learning of the majority of small children.

When we are very young the ability to arrange drawn marks on a page which visualise a particular scene or activity, accompanies the development of the skills required to use spoken language to express similar ideas and experiences. For the small child, simple drawing is a crucial way of interacting with the world. This occurs through making images; scribbles, scrawly circles, boxes and doodley waves all reflect the emerging knowledge of the world. The house, the family, the landscape start to appear and the marks made stand for things seen, remembered and imagined. This process is as essential as learning to speak and is also closely related to gaining language, where it is utterances rather than shapes and marks, which become the symbols of experience and knowledge. In our early years we all use art making to visualise experience and to share and communicate it.

Picasso goes on to say that the problem for the artist is how to remain creative as an adult. This is an issue for all, not just artists, if we view being creative as a wider experience. For all adults, on certain occasions, the opportunities for exploring and playing can remain as stimulating and as engaging as they ever were during those earliest times. Picasso describes this as a problem in that there is much that is different in the mind of an adult, and we cannot ever really go back to a genuinely childlike

29

experience. However, artists do need to reconnect to some of the qualities of simplicity, immediacy and perhaps a sense of relaxed 'unknowing' of what may happen, or at least a lack of worry that things may not work out as expected. These types of experiences can sometimes be difficult for adults and generally much easier for small children, but they are also essential for artists.

At the heart of both these early creative experiences and the work of mature artists is the process of using materials in various ways to make something that is new; one thing becomes another. The smallest child can create the image of a person from paper and coloured chalks; Rembrandt made portraits from linen, some pigments and sticky oil. There is a difference in the level of sophistication, but in both cases a process is used to change basic materials into artwork.

There is no doubt that there is a certain pleasure and satisfaction connected to this process regardless of age and experience. At times it can feel almost magical, converting what may often be such crude and rudimentary materials into something of significance. The small child's efforts might attain status and value within the family, and perhaps the best work will be posted on the fridge door for all to see each morning. Whereas the successful artist will gain greater cultural accolades and we know that sometimes the most extraordinary value can be attached to art work; for example the materials for a painting by Van Gogh would have cost very little, and yet reconfigured and worked by his hand some of his output is now worth millions.

For an artist to use various processes such as drawing, painting and making to transform materials into images and objects seems to be such a natural thing to do. Yet there is a certain mystery to how this comes about. Materials are changed far beyond the simple raw ingredients, images are formed and ideas and thoughts are also developed through this activity.

In a sense this is the way in which artists change the world. Not necessarily in a profound way, perhaps in quite a humble way; but nonetheless changes occur and after the work is completed the world is different as something new has been made.

These deliberate artistic acts are set against a background of much larger forces of transformation and change over which we have much less, or even no, control. It is part of the human condition to experience continual change both in nature and in the social world, whilst we value stability in our lives this is always set against considerable change and flux.

The most fundamental experiences of transformation and change to which we are subject are those of birth, growth, decay and death. There is a strong affinity between these natural cycles and the actions of creative artists, this can be viewed as an animating force at work within all specific art processes. Artists are concerned with the birth and growth of new forms and ideas and they use methods that promote change and diversity in their work to achieve this. Equally artists know that work can sometimes fail to develop well, resulting in lifeless images which they might discard and have to return to a task anew.

The idea that there is a quality of life in successful art is fundamental to the transformation of materials. Art is often judged on its vitality and the way in which it connects with an audience in a lively way.

There are often thoughts and conversations about work which artists and others may have which include phrases like 'it works', 'that's not quite working' or perhaps 'that works really well', this often involves other points and comments about the artwork. It is significant how unspecific these statements sometimes are and yet artists instinctively know what it means when something 'works'. Reflections such as these can acknowledge that a turning point has occurred in the process of development, and may be a recognition that there is indeed a certain quality of life appearing in the work. This moment could be reached quickly in a simple process, or it may be at the end of a long project and all artists try to recognise when this moment occurs.

There is always a technical element to these types of developments; for example printmaking or casting may be selected, but art processes are also imaginative and psychological. Many methods are not instant and this often allows work to be carried out over a long period of time. The artist's mind is active during the processing and development stages and the steps taken are accompanied by many judgements and decisions, which are both conscious and intuitive. Gradually the visual ideas are realised and developed into a physical form and the raw materials become animated as they become bound to the presence of successful images.

Decay and death may well be the end of cycles of transformation in the physical world. However, good art often survives us and the ability for strong creative work to transcend our human limitations is also a quality which we value greatly. We sometimes feel close to artists who inspire us, even if they are a long time dead, simply because their vision survives in their work. It seems that we can sometimes associate the distinct characteristics of another artist with the artwork they have made and a sense of identity can appear to emerge from it. This phenomenon is itself an interesting aspect of artistic transformation.

The fact that the work of small children can also contain such presence and a 'spark of life' indicates that this is something quite fundamental to our humanity. As the creative process occurs during the making of successful art and design there are many factors which come into play; no single explanation of the nature of this transformation will suffice, but the following sections seek to explore this from a number of different angles.

Think of a favourite meal which you yourself can prepare from a number of separate ingredients. How do you make it? What is the recipe for the best art that you make? Write down your art recipe by first listing the ingredients, not simply the materials but also the experiences which go into it, then describe the actions you take to transform these ingredients into successful images. Although this is personal to you, try to record this so clearly that someone else could follow the instructions.

Make a series of new images from an existing drawing as a starting point. Work aggressively, fearlessly and with exaggerated energy levels for a very short and previously decided amount of time, for example ten minutes on each one. Then hide the work away for a number of days and try to forget it completely. Later, pick a suitable time to develop and refine the images in a cool and relaxed frame of mind for a short but predetermined time on each, to bring them to completion. This is a simple timed strategy which puts together two quite different approaches. Self imposed rules can help avoid an over concern with finish and production at the expense of exploring new ideas.

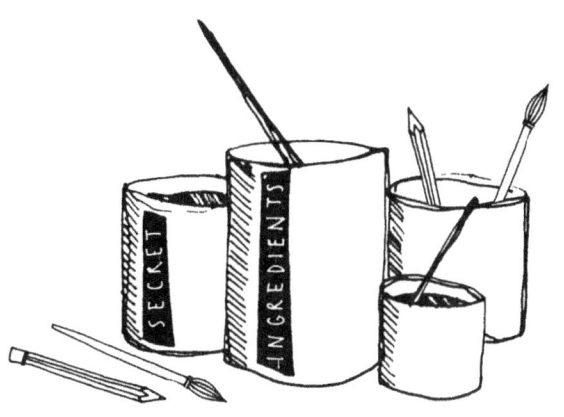

THE INTELLIGENCE OF MATERIALS

Materials are essential to the creation of artwork and as such they are also at the heart of an artist's relationship to the world. Each type of material has unique qualities and characteristics. This uniqueness does more than shape the appearance of what can be achieved, it allows visual artists to think in quite different ways and so offers great potential and possibilities.

I would go as far as to say that each material allows a different type of intelligence to become activated. To understand this we might first consider how other creative disciplines require different types of thinking. A dancer invents and thinks through the movement of a body in space, a mathematician through calculation and the use of numbers and an artist thinks through the manipulation of visual materials. If we take the example of the dancer, the mathematician and the artist, it is quite clear that the knowledge and experience of each allows them to use their intelligence quite distinctly; they do not think out the work they will do comprehensively in advance and then simply execute it. Whilst they may have some ideas at the start, it is the process of using their chosen materials, physical space and the body, numbers, or indeed a pen and paper, that allows the ideas to develop. These ideas are not abstract, because they rely on quite particular resources to become articulated. The type of thinking is also as unique as the materials.

Personally, I know that I cannot think like a dancer, neither can I think like a mathematician, but I can think like a visual artist and when I do this I tend to think through the use of materials. This is a key principle which can be applied to the range of materials an artist might select. It suggests that the choices made are more important that the look of the work or the skill required, rather it is the case that each material offers a way of working and thinking which is often quite unique.

There is for example, a world of difference between the use of three dimensional materials which can model and create form directly and the use of materials such as paint, which might create the illusion of a picture space which a viewer has to imagine. The classic division between painters and sculptors illustrates a striking difference in the way these artists might select materials which allow radically different approaches.

Beyond this the variations increase still further: a sculptor may model with clay, or carve into stone, a painter can rely on the freshness and immediacy of watercolour, or the gradually accrued depth and richness of the traditional use of oil paints. How different again is the thinking of a graphic artist using the combined impact of typography and images on a computer? It would be meaningless to ask the designer to work in oil paint for example, since each material has such distinctiveness and the demands of the thinking are also very different indeed.

This principle of the uniqueness of materials even applies at the level of simple choices for drawing, for example whether to choose a pen or a pencil, chalks or charcoal. Each material fosters a different type of thinking; a pen delineates form, charcoal can easily model the effects of light and so an artist may start to relate the world quite differently depending on the material used.

Since these substances are so important in showing how a relationship to the world is conceived, explored and developed, there is always an emotional relationship which connects artists strongly to their different materials. I have seen artists get unusually excited by scrap pieces of metal, unformed lumps of clay and even by the colour and texture of paint when it is still in the jar. This type of reaction is fairly common for artists.

Artists enjoy a vital relationship with these very particular and highly varied resources and the sight and feel of materials has two key dimensions from the start. Firstly there is the simple sensual enjoyment of the substance in its own right; this might range from brittle and dusty sticks of black charcoal to the blooms and runny washes of inks. Every material has a unique charm. Secondly, the artist looks at the material and is excited by a sense of potential. The imagination starts to fire and we want to make something; we want to explore the potential of the material and mental images may also begin to form alongside the desire to start to work.

I am not suggesting an overly sentimental attitude or a poetic experience. The initial response can be quite pragmatic since the recognition of the potential of the materials is a first step to the creation of new possibilities. However, there are a variety of emotional characteristics to this connection. Firstly, the artist gives attention to materials, noticing and exploring their qualities. Secondly, this is developed through contact and interaction, and thirdly, a quality of care or even love for the materials is present. These aspects of attention, contact and care are present in our key human relationships; the connection between the artist and the material is a powerful analogue of this and can reveal dimensions of the artist's 'interior' or psychological experience. This is true not only for the positive feelings, since materials and their behaviour, once creative work is underway, can also cause frustration, anger and disappointment just as certainly as joy and surprise. Staring into a paint pot, marvelling at the colour and enjoying the smell is really just the start.

When artists make a choice to use a particular material they are also partaking in a tradition, since every material has a history. This is an important part of the specific nature of materials. The basic properties may well dictate certain uses; large scale sculptures are not generally made from oil paint for example. The potential of a material in the hands of an artist is always fed by a growing knowledge of what others have achieved with similar materials before. In fact, this is essential.

Every instance of visual art and design through painting, drawing, sculpture, new media, graphics, fashion design and illustration etc., stands as a discrete example of the limitless potential of materials. So the contact with materials and the relationship which is developed, depend both on the direct practice of making and also on seeing, discovering and thinking in the presence of the work of others. The use of materials is the physical location of strong artistic connections which exert an imaginative pull on the mind of the artist whilst work is underway.

Artists will have ideas in their heads, but they will be undeveloped and can seemingly evaporate and disappear unless they are explored in a 'physical form'. Everything from an incidental doodle on the back of an envelope to a classical Greek sculpture depends on specific materials to allow the image to become visible to ourselves and others. Materials shape the possibilities offered to the artist in the making of the work and they also embody the final form in the world, affecting how viewers encounter and experience it.

Much visual art capitalises on the closeness a viewer can experience to the materials and the process of making. Sometimes this is one of the reasons that, however good a reproduction is, it is not as rich an experience as seeing the real thing. This quality may be especially strong in art made with traditional materials which can display a record of the making in the detail of their surfaces. For example the undisguised brushwork of a Rembrandt portrait, presents a powerful connection to the sequence of mark making and the building up of a strong image. There are other artists who have used materials in quite minimal ways, for whom these qualities seems much less evident. Carl Andre's series of sculptures made with arrangements of fire bricks (1966 Equivalent VIII, Tate Modern, London) are a good example. However, with such art although it is simpler, or sometimes precisely because it is simpler, the specific materials remain a major part of work's identity. Even work of the modern and post-modern era where industrial manufacturing processes might be used by artists, or if the recycling of found objects is important, then the response to and use of materials is no less significant. The physical properties are fundamental in all these cases, regardless of the extraordinary range of ideas, intentions and vastly different contexts. Even conceptual work, which proposes qualities of 'nothing' as its focus, depends on quite a lot of 'something' to appear as artwork; in this case a spartan and stripped down gallery space may also form an important part of the presence of the work.

41

As artists we grow to love our materials, just as an expert cook is passionate about raw ingredients. We can become intimately familiar with them, test them out, find out their normal range and perhaps how they behave when pushed to explore their limits. Artists often put one material with another to combine them and see what happens. Both simple and complex combinations can be explored, to discover if the results of such experiments can move work forward in a good way. Artists also value the 'messes' and disasters, as this is all part of the experience of building a repertoire and developing knowledge of the full potential of materials.

There is a very long tradition in art where artists use materials which are sometimes difficult to control, substances that smudge, run or flow, or combine in unexpected ways. For many artists there is an evident delight in this unpredictability; it seems to connect very directly with an experimental attitude of mind. To work in this way requires a certain level of confidence. For the developing artist this confidence depends on a realisation that not only 'mistakes are ok', but more significantly that the unexpected error can be worked with productively. Art materials do throw up the unexpected; this is often the nature of working with them. It is not so much that they are difficult to control, more perhaps that we value their capacity to surprise us. As artists we do not control materials; we interact with them and in many special and unique ways we think through this interaction. In order to do this, artists also welcome unexpected results as work progresses, since this makes for a living relationship with materials, one in which there is both give and take.

Get close to your materials. Before starting work on a charcoal drawing snap some pieces. Crush, crumble and smudge them, smell them, think of the willow, the bundled twigs and the charring process, burning without burning up. It is important to get to know your materials and their properties intimately, so that they become second nature and give great flexibility in all that you do.

Explore an existing image with a series of radical changes of scale and materials; for example make much larger images (or objects) with a variety of combined materials, then work very small with the same variety of combined materials. In each of these really push what can be achieved when these materials are worked with together. Repeat this process using single materials and now work with a sense of reduction and purity. These processes can allow images to change and develop with ease, but don't be cautious, make the large images really big and the small really small, then review the work as a set to consider next steps.

Put two images, or parts of images together to make a third; create this new third image with materials not used in the previous two. This is basic but at the heart of experimental artistic method.

Make a series of images using a material that is new to you; expand your range and your repertoire.

Have a go at making an image using a material that you know you dislike. Force it to work for you, get cross if necessary but follow it through to a conclusion. What are the reasons for this dislike? Does it not suit your style? If so, change your style to suit the material.

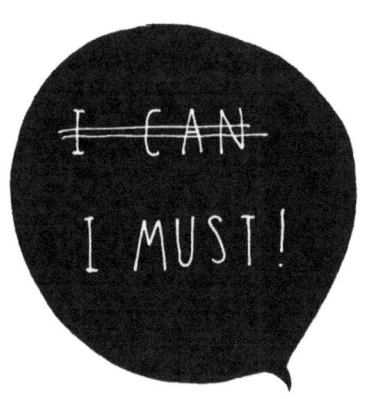

Artistic Skills

The musician Arnold Schoenberg writing in 1911 on the problems of teaching art stated:

> I believe art is born of 'I must', not of 'I can'. A craftsman 'can'.... What he wants to do he can do – good and bad, shallow and profound, new-fangled and old-fashioned – he can! But the artist must. He has no say in the matter, it is nothing to do with what he wants; but since he must he also can. Perhaps he was not born with something; then he acquires it.[6]

This quote reveals something fundamental about the nature of artistic skill. All artistic production, creative transformations and the successful use of materials depend upon skill. Creativity and skill are related; however they are certainly not the same thing. To illustrate this Schoenberg describes the application of skill as being neutral in value, resulting in work that can be good or bad though nonetheless highly skilled. This is clear when we think of work which may have very high production qualities. It could be a movie, a piece of sculpture or a

---

6   Schoenberg, Style and Idea, p. 365.

building, anything in fact where a great deal of skill has gone into the making of the work. However, such work may sometimes be quite dull, predictable and ultimately very unsatisfying as creative work, despite the level of technical skill required to make it. The reverse is also true; sometimes creative work can be moving, highly communicative and profound, even if the skill level of the artist is not that high. Skill is connected with the handling of the media and materials but it is not the message. The very highest points of artistic endeavour often occur where we see the skills and communication combined in extraordinary ways.

Schoenberg also introduces the notion that there is a drive for an artist to produce which seems to come from within. In this respect skills are acquired to support the impulse to create and not as an end in their own right.

As artists we may wish to acquire new skills and to develop the ones we possess; perhaps we see things to aspire to but cannot yet achieve. Creative ambitions can be frustrated if we lack skills we need and sometimes we have to work hard to acquire them. Learning an art skill usually requires a process to be demonstrated in some way, also to see good completed examples, and then personal practise is needed in order to gain ability. The level of rehearsal required for the highest levels of achievement can be considerable. For many an education in the arts is a very good beginning, but beyond this, regular work is required to embed and develop specific abilities. Research into learning has indicated that, across a wide range of creative and performance disciplines, the very highest achievers have often practised to develop their skills for around four hours per day for at least ten years[7]. There are rarely exceptions to this, so commitment and dedication have a clear part to play.

There is however a complexity to the possession of skills that can sometimes have an unexpected impact on the development of artistic creativity. This is because the ability to use a particular skill extremely well, for example to draw very realistically, can sometimes impact negatively on the flexibility required to move forward and to develop new skills. Sometimes an individual skill appears to be 'hardwired' and almost too dominant and it can inhibit the development of new possibilities. At the simplest level those who are good at being neat and precise may need to develop skills in working roughly and boldly, and those who are good at being rough and bold may also need to acquire the skills to work with precision. It is important to develop a skill repertoire but for some this can feel uncomfortable, particularly those who have already invested a great deal of time acquiring a very definite skill set. This usually applies more strongly to artists who enjoy precision, since high levels of control are being explored successfully and it often feels more difficult for them to explore 'less controlled' approaches. The courage to take this step is definitely worth it.

Different artists may have strengths in different areas of skill. Why this is so usually depends on a mix of prior experience and sometimes an innate disposition or preference for particular approaches. Some people are good at fine graphic detail, others at using beautiful combinations of colour, handling three-dimensional materials, or producing strong compositions. In my experience most skills can be learned if a choice is made

---

7   Ericsson et al. Psychological Review.

and the confidence is there to do so. Acquiring new skills always depends to an extent on building upon what one can already do. Often we are drawn to mastering skills that seem to suit us, ones perhaps that fit in with our developing abilities. By studying how others have developed these skills and then by trying things out ourselves, it is possible to learn a great deal and also to eventually achieve at a high level. In the same way that a child learns the complexities of speech, encouragement and imitation is fundamental to the acquisition of all skills. These abilities are developed gradually but as Schoenburg indicates, it is what is done with them, what is made and created, which counts.

Art skills are often characterised as technical abilities and this is clearly important. However there are more generic 'learning skills' that also underpin strong creativity. Successful artists and designers are also very good at learning as they adapt and continually change in order to move their work forward. The American educationalist Roger Schank[8] has outlined three major skill groups which support successful learning. I have amended his suggestions a little to link them more closely to learning in the visual arts.

CONCEPTUAL SKILLS

Predicting – Anticipating the likely outcome of particular actions. This affects choices and decision making at every step of the way as new work is generated.

Modelling – This is the ability to construct a mental image of the possible result of a process or technique.

Experimenting – To try out different approaches and ideas in

---

8   Schank, The Twelve Cognitive Processes that Underlie Learning.

order to discover which are the most effective. This is also linked to risk-taking and is discussed more fully in part two.

Evaluation – To be able to reflect on the merits of creative work, to seek and to perceive the value of complex ideas and processes.

ANALYTIC SKILLS

Diagnosis and Causation – The ability to look at a problem or challenge and to see relationships. This might encompass technique, organisation, or the wider demands of a project.

Planning – Learning to plan using both rational conscious thought and also including the space for intuitive steps along the way. Advance planning sets the conditions for success; resourcing and organising are included within this phase of the work.

Judging – Schank describes this as an objective skill. In art and design this is linked to evaluation; it involves the ability to step back from completed work and to try to 'call it like it is', to identify the strengths and the weaknesses. This skill also applies to our analysis of the work of others and is an important part of developing our response to it.

SOCIAL SKILLS

Influencing – In visual arts this applies to the effect work has on an audience. It also involves the ability to understand the views of others, to empathise and then to be able to engage and persuade. Influencing through conversation and discussion with others is part of this too.

Teamworking – Creative projects often involve extended teams. Being effective in teams, adapting to different roles, sometimes including leadership, is an essential skill. It is difficult to get far without this.

- Negotiating – Linked to influencing and teamwork, this is the ability to strike a balanced deal, to help resolve differences of opinions and ideas and so to play a part in moving projects on productively.
- Describing – To be able to articulate a view, to verbally outline a plan, an idea, a vision and to describe this to others is very much part of the social skill set for a creative artist.

This summary of abilities which underlie some of the more traditional notions of artistic skill covers a wide range and individuals may have skills that are weighted in different areas, as development occurs gradually as we grow and mature. Just as developing a specific art skill often requires a deliberate choice to step beyond what may feel comfortable, so these aspects of creativity grow more quickly when challenges are taken up and there is the confidence to take a risk. The implication of this may well be that creative people often have a certain resilience to failure and the ability to learn from it.

Review three pieces of work that you hold as some of the best things you have achieved so far. To what extent is this work the result of a particular skill set? Make a list of your art skills and a wish list of how you would like to develop. Plan some new work that will help take you in this direction.

Do something badly. Deconstruct a skill so that you take it back through formative stages; this might feel difficult, awkward, clumsy and ill-judged. Imagine you are less than you are, work at a low level, let go of the notion of skill, but still try to address your creative concerns. In this way habits of crafted and styled images will not get in the way and a new view of your ideas might arise.

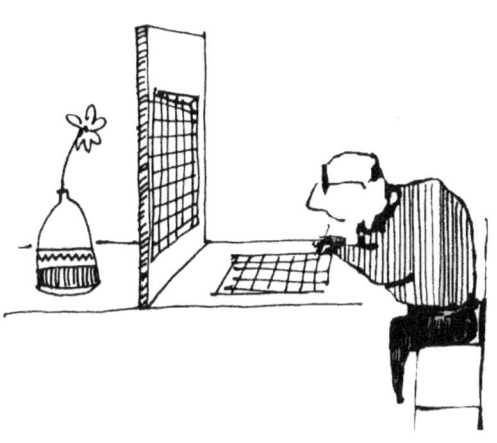

Drawing to Generate

Drawing can be viewed as a primary means of expression for the very young and to a degree it seems to play this role for artists too, as drawing can be so direct, immediate and responsive. Simple materials and mark-making facilitate this as drawing often plays a key role in handling the beginnings of ideas and projects.

However, for mature artists, drawing takes on different functions beyond the way in which a small child might test and discover a relationship with the world. Drawing can become much more complex and varied and it is also quite difficult to define as it is not a singular activity. Cooking is a good analogy since just as a chef can boil, roast, sauté, stir-fry, stew, bake etc., there are a multitude of ways to go about drawing. Drawing is a whole collection of methods and approaches.

In 1967 the sculptor Richard Serra constructed a list of verbs which he then went on to enact in the creation of new work. The purpose of this list was to act as a guide for generating form. It had over one hundred entries and began as follows: 'to roll, to crease, to fold, to store, to bend, to shorten, to twist' and so on. Each of these activities was subsequently explored as a starting point using a variety of raw materials. For a mature artist the activity of drawing has a lot in common with such a list, since drawing is more often concerned with 'generation' rather than 'expression'. Drawing is generative in that it often provides the initial connection to the world and to visual ideas, which can then be built on and developed.

To illustrate the range of approaches it is also possible to create a list of verbs, all of which describe possible drawing activities, as well as indications of the purpose such drawings might have. For example:

to map	*to analyse*
to measure	*to mystify*
to record	*to intrigue*
to visualise	*to shock*
to observe	*to amuse*
to imagine	*to question*
to form	*to explain*
to explore	*to repeat*
to scrawl	*to decorate*
to deface	*to embellish*
to doodle	*to experiment*
to plan	*to test*
to illustrate	*to layer*
to invent	*to delineate*
to compose	*to shade*
to arrange	*to texture*
to question	*to engrave*
to persuade	*to drip*
to instruct	*to scrape*
to define	*to rub*

Such a list prompts thoughts about both the methods and approaches involved, and also the impact that a drawing might create. This range and flexibility often contributes to the early stages of creative work, as it helps shape the conditions where ideas can connect in rich and sometimes unexpected ways.

Whilst artists and designers have always made drawings, the status of this activity has experienced changes. It is often the case that drawing supports more major work; it is part of the creative method of arriving at a final result. The great building, sculpture or painting may well have many drawings which supported its development, but these drawings perhaps remain hidden away in books and drawers. As such, drawing tends to be a less visible and quite private activity. In more recent times the interest in creative methods of artists has led to a surge in interest in artists' drawings. This can be fascinating where a wide range of options and ideas, many of which have been rejected, are revealed in this more temporary and ephemeral work. Since drawing is the most immediate tool to visualise and respond to the seeds of an idea, it can sometimes feel like an insight into the very heart of a creative process.

Drawing gives form to ideas through what is sometimes viewed as a type of visual 'language', and although it functions quite differently from text or spoken language, rather like words drawings also explore conventions and 'idioms'. Things seen, remembered and imagined can be created as clear representations or variations and distortions, or as plans, diagrams, maps, doodles or other freely improvised abstractions.

Drawing has its own set of specific conventions and methods, many of which capitalise on simplicity and the desire to create form quickly and effectively and whilst drawing can be extremely varied, it is useful to consider some categories into which many approaches fall.

Line drawing is perhaps the most basic and fundamental. It is how our earliest drawings were made: lines are used to draw the shapes of the things we see. This is a widely used convention which we often accept quite blindly; interestingly the visual world rarely contains any lines at all, only edges where one thing begins and another starts. In drawing, lines are used to mark the edges of things, where the boundaries of tones change and shapes are seen.

Lines can also be used to describe surfaces in the form of contours. Contour drawings are linked to the way in which coverings such as clothing may enwrap form. This connects closely with the appearance of clothing where the folds and surface textures reveal the form of a body within. This can be applied to many types of subject as artists use line to trace and wrap surfaces, to rebuild form and to describe the contours of three dimensional shapes. The drawings of Henry Moore, Giacometti or Dürer are good examples of this approach. The convention of representing the height of landscape with contour lines on maps is comparable to this too.

As soon as groups of marks are made, the effects of light and dark become a factor. The representation of tone is less of an invented convention because this is closely linked to optical experience. Very little of what we see directly involves clear lines, but all of it is constructed by the effect of light and shadow to reveal forms and relationships. The best materials to work with to explore these qualities are of course less linear ones and smudgy charcoal, putty rubber or black and white chalks are ideal.

Line, contour and tone are clear and quite formal broad categories; they are useful ways to consider some basic approaches which are subject to a huge amount of variation. To extend this thinking further in the direction of creativity it is useful to consider the notion of 'gesture'.

Gesture is connected to the particular qualities of the marks which are made. The word 'gestural' is often used to refer to drawings of a certain type. A gestural drawing or even a single gestural mark is usually understood as something where the physical movement used to create it has a high energy, as the marks made seem to sweep across the surface, or maybe stab about and twist around. In these cases the work is sometimes considered to be more expressive than restrained, perhaps because the effect is bold and forthright and reveals a certain type of confidence on the part of the artist. However, what is presented by the quality of the marks made is often more complex and subtle than this.

Most drawings are made with gestures and created by the movement of the hand and the contact with the surface on which marks are made. The specific quality of these gestures may well be energetic, big and bold, but equally they may be restrained, small and tightly focused. These marks are on one hand required to give form to an image; on the other, they are also evidence of the distinct quality of an individual's creative approach.

The marks made and the way they come together may have a very personal quality and a style which has a unique or 'autographic' nature. The fact that drawing materials are usually simple, direct and responsive recorders of gestures helps this. Drawings often possess a strong identity and a quality of 'live' visual thought which is revealed in part by how the marks are actually made. This immediacy can present qualities that may not be present in major art work which has been more crafted and developed.

Drawings can reveal aspects of temperament and disposition in a similarly direct way. In the modern era much has been made of the link between personality and creativity, an attitude fuelled by 19th century Romanticism and the notion of 'individual genius'. It is in simple drawings perhaps more than anywhere else, that it is possible to witness a connection to highly specific and individual qualities, although we do not need to be a genius for this to be the case. Beyond the actual content or subject matter of a drawing, the style and the way in which gestures are made can reveal a great deal. Gesture embodies the quality of the 'energy' in a drawing, for example whether a drawing is contem-plative, analytic, aggressive, lyrical, workmanlike or hesitant. It is important to be alive to these types of possibilities in both appreciating and creating drawings and for individual artists the quality of a drawing may also change, due to the needs and intentions of a task.

For many young artists learning to draw 'well' and to really make good use of this key creative skill is a significant aim. Some may be anxious about their abilities and skill levels generally and because of its place as a central artistic activity, drawing is often a particular concern. Building skills in drawing can involve a significant amount of work from direct observa-tion. To record proportion and structure with clarity and accu-racy is a significant challenge and the development of these abilities may take many years. Initially most very small children will feel that all drawings are good and any notion of a skill level is pretty much irrelevant. It is the years which follow, co-inciding with early schooling, when getting things to 'look right' becomes important. During this phase there is a mix of harder and softer options with which children might work, natural organic forms are pretty forgiving if unintended distortions creep in while landscapes, objects and environments with clear structure can present more difficulties. It is the human figure which is the most demanding, since even slight distortions, if unintended, can arouse dissatisfaction because the effect is so unlike the observed appearance. There is much to learn which can help develop skills in proportion and structure and techniques of measurement and perspective will support this type of development.

However, whilst 'getting it to look right' is an important learning stage, if such realism was the only aim and we consider where this would lead, we can see that this is only a part of the story.

When drawing in response to observation, a sense of optical realism is an important component; but even when a drawing has this approach as a main aim, the exploration of materials, marks and the quality of response is always significant. A suitable analogy here would be to consider how a computer programme might play back a music score with perfect pitch, timing and absolute consistency time and again, yet this experience in its perfection is sterile. In handmade observed drawing there is huge scope to include and play with the variable qualities of expression, exploration and response which is missing from this type of 'correct' but mechanical approach. Just as a jazz ensemble invents and creates experiences through the process of playing, it is also possible for observed drawing to be equally lively and playful.

The drawings of Rodin, Schiele, Kollwitz and Van Gogh provide us with celebrated examples which give a full flavour of the scope and range possible purely within the category of 'observed' drawing. In these examples the quality of gesture not only reveals the human and autographic nature of drawing, but is harnessed to communicate an emotional connection to the subject matter. The things seen by the artist are distorted and changed in order to present the viewer with a more emotional and psychological experience of the world; this is achieved through a type of playing with initial visual experience. Such examples reveal the power of expressive communication which can be achieved through drawing alone.

The acquisition of this type of high level skill is certainly dependent on practice. A key part of this is evaluation and reflection and for many artists this is helped by the keeping of drawing books. Many artists highly value their drawing books because they offer a record of how images and ideas develop which can easily be reviewed and revisited. This is where drawings which are perhaps the most fleeting of visual notes can gather; sometimes if the marks were not made then the image would be gone and forgotten; where many small drawings exist together ideas can quickly build in resonance and significance. Sometimes artists have to think quickly, drawing can be an effective record of this process and often quite humble technical pieces can support the development of strong and exciting ideas. In such drawing books, artists can exploit the lowly convenience of simple materials.

Does an artist have to be good at drawing? I think the answer is definitely yes, as this skill is so often at the heart of an artist's visual relationship to the world.

Address some new work by starting with a non-stop drawing hour. Make as many of the following drawings in just sixty minutes as you can: records of what you can see, imagine, remember, doodle, create diagrams, illustrations, make invisible drawings in the air and draw maps of where you are physically and conceptually. Work a little too quickly to think very much about it and ensure you complete all the tasks. Place the work together, look for links between pieces and also reflect on the differences. This strategy can open up unexpected possibilities.

Make a drawing which uses the greatest possible variety of line thickness, but no tone. Make a drawing which uses the greatest possible variety of tone, but no lines.

Make a series of drawings only using curved lines; repeat but only use straight lines this time.

Make a series of abstract drawings of simple marks and rhythms which record conversations between a group of friends as they actually happen; draw the 'sounds' not the words and record their locations in space as they occur over time.

Use a drawing book to make a small but important drawing each day, spend no more than fifteen minutes on each one and continue for a complete calendar month. As this develops allow your mind to anticipate and reflect on this work, the passage of time each day is heading toward this activity. Take your visual ideas to this task each day.

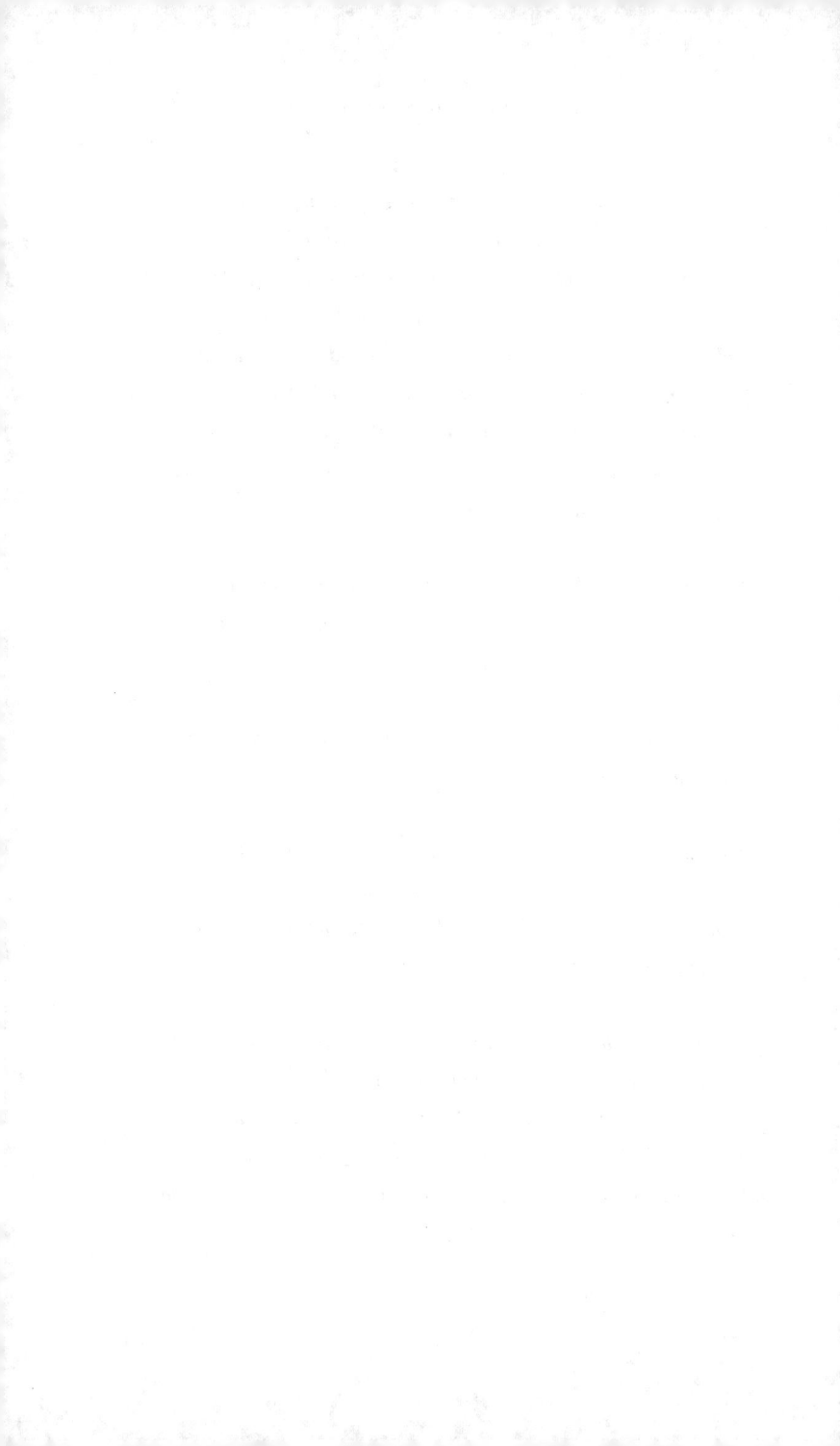

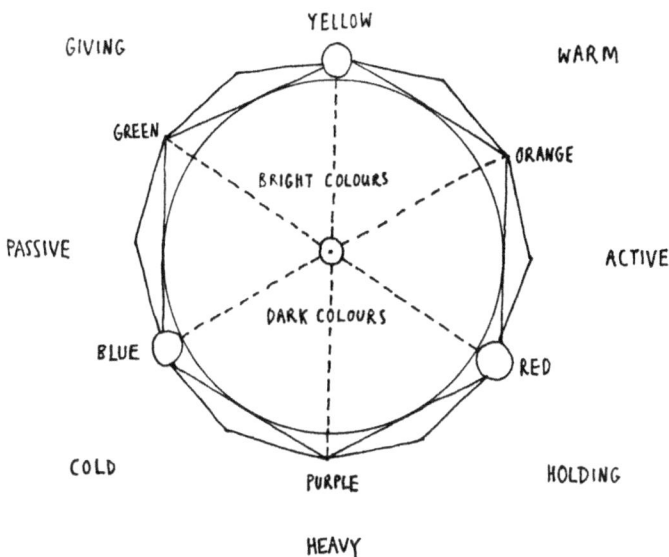

LIGHT

GIVING   WARM

YELLOW

GREEN   ORANGE

BRIGHT COLOURS

PASSIVE   ACTIVE

DARK COLOURS

BLUE   RED

COLD   HOLDING

PURPLE

HEAVY

Colour

Colour can be viewed as a basic or formal element of art making, together with line, tone, shape, texture and volume. This type of thinking has been strongly influenced by the logic of the teaching of the Bauhaus design school in 1920s Germany and it is still a key idea in Western art education in the 21st Century. However, to see colour as simply another component of image making could cause us to overlook its unique power and status in creative work. Colour is truly elemental to our experience of the world and for artists it offers the possibility of shaping the response of an audience in fundamental ways. Elemental qualities and colours sit well together; the red of blood, fire and heat, the blue of the sky and the yellow of the sun. Alongside these traditional primaries the 19th century chemist Wilhelm Ostwald also proposed sea-green as a fourth 'proto-colour' as a signifier of the natural organic world.

Science has greatly contributed to our understanding of colour and since Newton published his treatise on the behaviour of light and colour in 1704, a variety of models have been created to illustrate it. The beginning of the 20th century saw the first standardised colour system designed by Alfred Munsell which was adopted to quantify soil research in the USA. Munsell developed a model of a 'colour solid' which described colour in three dimensions; these measures were value, light to dark, chroma, the saturation or intensity of the colour, and hue, the specific colour e.g. red or green. Later, with the emergence of 20th century printing technology, the system of mixing cyan, magenta, yellow and black allowed the mass production of realistic coloured images and the Pantone colour matching system also allowed printers and designers to categorise colours accurately. New technologies have seen monitors and printers which are capable of differentiating colours to an extraordinarily complex degree; whereas the Pantone system defined 1,114 separate colours, a basic computer monitor can now identify millions of separate colour variations. These contemporary digital displays use 'colour spaces' to define colour, which is a three dimensional model based on Munsell's original definitions.

In the Bauhaus the teachers successfully combined both a technical and also a more poetic stance toward colour. Johannes Itten and Josef Albers took up an analytic approach often creating images which directly explored interesting optical effects, whereas Vassily Kandinsky was influential through his highly improvised exploration of the relationship between colour, music and spiritual experience.

A knowledge of colour mixing and behaviour is important to artists, but the power of colour to communicate and to influence an audience usually depends less on an intellectual understanding and much more on emotional and intuitive responses. For many artists and designers colour is a continual challenge which possesses great potential. The painter John Constable once said that he hoped to 'preserve God Almighty's daylight' and for any creative colourist the problem is similar as colour, like daylight, is never a fixed experience; colour is always on the move and in a state of flux. This is true both optically and psychologically.

Artists benefit greatly from acquiring knowledge about colour; however the lived experience of colour complicates and can confound any notion of a quantifiable system. The associations we bring to our experience of colour go way beyond the basic elemental identifications; our ability to ascribe meaning to colour is complex and rich and is often rooted in our social and cultural experience. Black as an absence of colour can stand for death in Western cultures, yet in Eastern cultures the colour of death is white. Red might stand for fire and blood, or maybe courage, sex, Communism or the Holy Spirit. In his book *Chroma* the film maker and artist Derek Jarman gives a highly personal account of colour which presents deeply considered descriptions of these associations. Whole chapters are devoted to single colours. This is a short section reflecting on the nature of red:

Red is a moment in time. Blue constant. Red is quickly spent. An explosion of intensity. It burns itself. Disappears like fiery sparks into the gathering shadow. To warm ourselves in the long dark winter when the red has departed. We welcome robin redbreast, and the red berries that sustain life. Dress in the Coco Cola red of Santa Claus the bringer of gifts. We sit round the table and sing 'The holly bears a berry as bright as any blood.' Our winter faces are dyed a cheerful red. We preserve the red like a flame. Life is red. Red is for the living, but the scarlet berry of the yew poisons, keeps the devils at bay in the churchyard.[9]

---

9   Jarman, Chroma, p. 37.

This quote presents a powerful view of our emotional experience of colour. The appearance of the colour circle, with the fanned out primaries and orange, green and purple in-between, shows the formal relationships, how to mix colours and the relative position of warm and cool hues; but it tells us nothing of how we live with colour. Jarman offers an invitation to feel what colour means to us and for any artist this is a key consideration. The lived experience of colour, which is to a high degree a social and imaginative experience, is for the artist an exciting possibility in creative work. Yet we cannot dismiss the knowledge of colour interaction and formal organisation as somehow being separate from this more emotional perspective; the complexity of colour requires us to explore it on many fronts. Itten's eloquent model of the artists' colour circle can help us to understand how these two important aspects are intertwined.

Itten illustrates the familiar colour circle with some descriptive text. Light and heavy, bright and dark, warm and cool, passive and active, also the verbs 'to have' and 'to give' are all positioned at specific points around and within the circle[10]. The design presents a system of oppositions and tensions, an almost Karmic vision where the colour circle becomes a symbol of balance; the light yellow rising from the heaviness of purple, the warmth of the yellowy orange set against the chill of blue, the active principle of red-orange against the passive power of blue green. Itten indentifies the range of red-violet as colour which possesses and holds with great strength (*erhaben*), like the warm dark of night and sleep perhaps; this is set against the yellow-

---

10   see illustration p67

72

green of fresh spring leaves and growth, colour that serves and 'gives' of itself to the world (*ergeben*).

These opposites seem to make some sense, as they create a bridge between the formal organisation of colour relationship and the wider experiences and associations which colour can create.

The model of oppositions also links to the physiological experience of colour and the behaviour of our eyes and how we react to the pure sensation of colour.

Within our eyes, coloured light is a stimulant and it excites the cone cells of our retina. We know what it is to be temporarily blinded by bright light when the after image of the glanced at sun persists. Likewise the removal of red tinted glasses causes the experience of colour to be distorted; the whole world briefly appears to turn to luminous greens. A simple experiment can be conducted by staring at a small square of saturated red colour on a white background for one minute. Quickly replace this with pure white only, but continue to stare and a ghostly after-image will appear. Red creates a glowing turquoise effect, yellow becomes magenta and blue translates to a warm yellow. These after-images appear as a type of luminous glow not at all like reflected colour. The relationship between the original colour and that of the afterimage is set by the stimulation of the separate red, green and blue sensing cone cells within the eye. The sudden removal of the saturated red results in a relatively stronger signal being sent to the brain by the green and blue cones, hence the illusion of a turquoise glow appears.

For the artist this experience is significant because the pure sensations of colour have a powerful and physically exciting effect.

There are many examples in art and design where single areas of strong colour dominate visual experience especially in the decorative design of products, interiors and fabrics. In the 1950's colour field painters such as Barnett Newman and Mark Rothko explored this approach and, in the 1960s, Yves Klein patented his International Blue producing super saturated plain and textured surfaces. These artists often placed areas of different colour together to create striking effects. We sometimes speak of 'beautifully orchestrated' colour, as if combinations of colour can present an almost musical effect, rather like groups of distinct musical instruments coming together to create a richly integrated experience.

It is the impact of colours in combination which so often engages artists. Control of colour is complex since in combination they genuinely do 'interact' optically due to how our eyes behave. Josef Albers published a book with a set of visual samples called the Interaction of Colour which is a comprehensive exploration of these effects. With the use of simple shapes and a series of overlapping coloured cards, Albers demonstrated that colour perception actually changes depending on how one colour is set against another. These effects are often most noticeable when highly saturated colour is set against subtle coloured or 'chromatic' greys; for example, a saturated orange can appear to 'pull' the blue from a cool grey as it makes the grey appear more blue than if it were set against white. Many artists who are strong colourists exploit the effects of colour interaction; the vibrant impact of work by Pierre Bonnard, or Fra Angelico for example, depends on a skilful exploitation of this knowledge. The effect of this is to create a sense of animation, a vibrant and literally 'vibrating' optical life. This animation of colour is for many an integral part of the life of an image. Adrian Stokes, the English artist and writer on art, speaks directly of colour being alive in certain images: 'colour is inside, like the blood which comes to fullness in the lips, lights and vivifies the skin.'[11]

The optical effect of colour is not an isolated physical reaction which is separate from the more poetic associative experience of colour. Stokes' quote invites us to make a strong link between our own body and the animating power of colour in art, between the energy of the complex vibrations of coloured light and how we connect with this in both a physical and affective way.

The sensation of colour in art creates experiences which are fundamentally human. We experience the visual energy of light and this is complex and sometimes unpredictable at a physiological level; colour also energises our imaginative response to things seen through the powerful associations it brings in its wake. This is the nature of the opportunity which colour offers to the artist and why colour is such a potent consideration in the creation of any piece of art work.

Transform the development of any piece of work midway by deliberately using the 'wrong' colours; with care and thought choose totally inappropriate colours. This does not mean a simple reversal but try to choose colour that goes totally against how you would normally make decisions. This may seem deliberately destructive, but it is not so since this action may help you question assumptions and see new possibilities.

---

11 Stokes, Colour and Form, p. 43.

Make an abstract image about an actual emotional experience you remember clearly. Use the effects of the marks, shapes and especially the colour, to conjure up and recreate the quality of the remembered emotion. Try to move beyond the way colour associates to mood in a general way; be as specific to your own feelings as you can. Be prepared to allow the image to take on its own identity as you work; treat it as a dialogue that can grow, not simply an illustration of a feeling.

Make an image which is a tribute to the best ideas of an artist whom you feel uses colour really well. Imagine they become you for a while; let what you know and feel about their work guide your actions and really get into the spirit of how they use colour. This is more than an exercise, more like a fundamental process, learning by playful imitation.

PART II

DEVELOPING

CREATIVITY

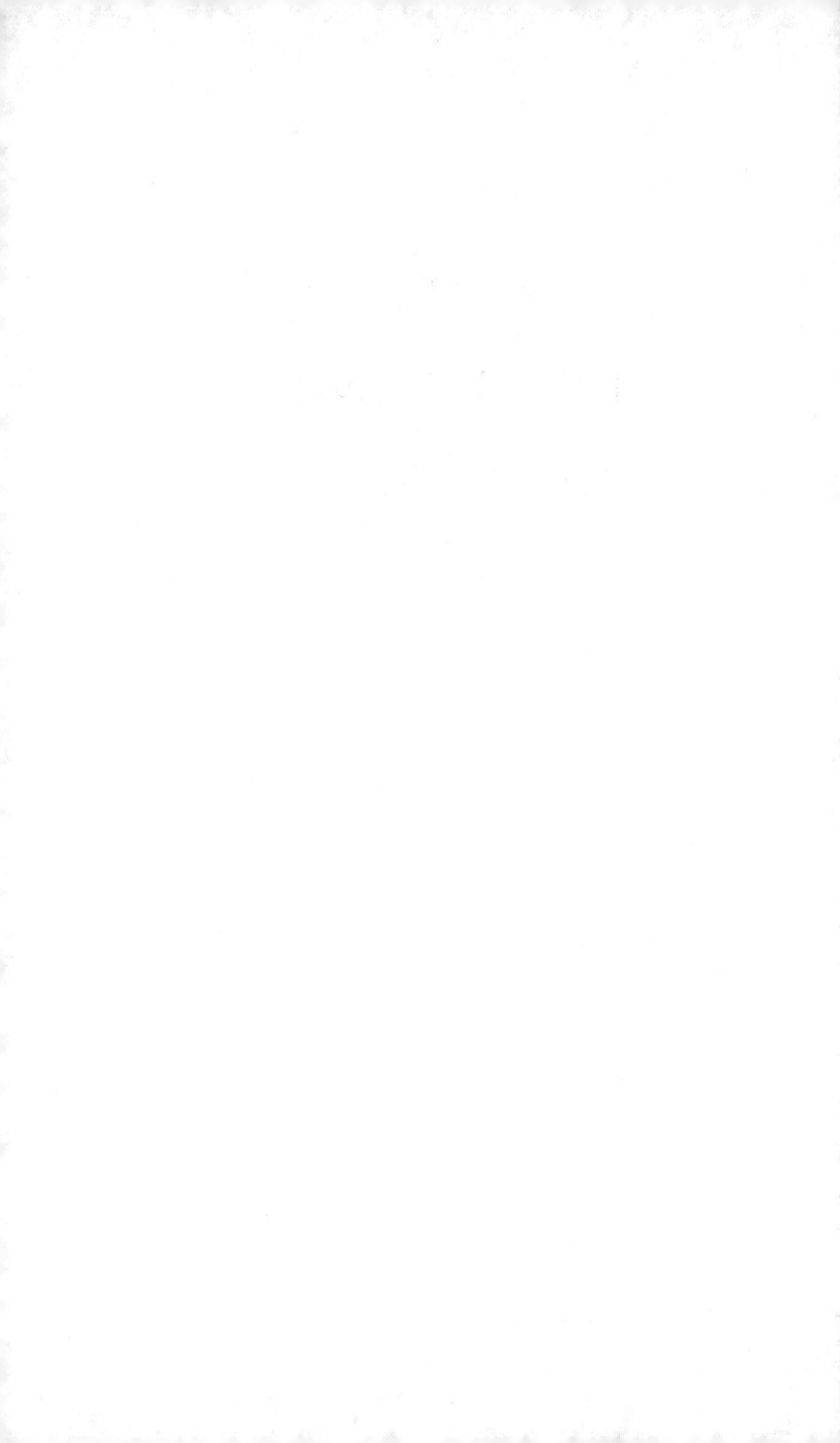

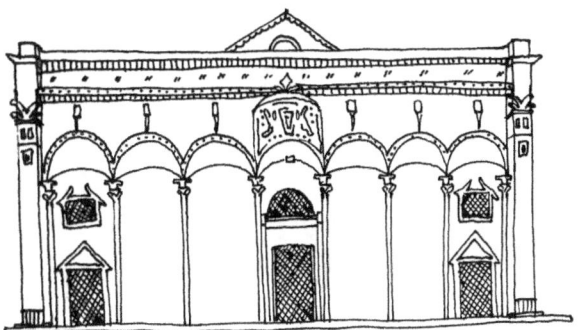

THE SYMBOLIC WORLD

At the northern end of the square of Santissima Annunziata in Florence is the beautiful church after which the square is named. It is a striking place both architecturally and because of the significance of its contents. The façade consists of an open loggia with seven plain but elegant arches, the central one covering the main doors of the church. Although it is in the middle of the old town and right next to Brunelleschi's famous Hospital of the Innocents, the design of which the loggia mirrors, it is less visited than many other Florentine art history venues and is still very much a functional religious building used by the local community.

The visitor enters via a pair of heavy wooden doors, as one might in many Italian churches, but unusually the space opens immediately to a quite empty colonnaded cloister. The centre of this area is open to the light and although there is now a simple glazed roof, originally this would have been completely uncovered. The architectural work here is that of Michelozzo (1396-1472) and it is a small treasure of Renaissance design based on repeated cubes and semi-circular arches and vaults. It expresses a clear mathematical order and rhythm throughout and there is a notable precision, restraint and brightness to the overall space.

The main body of the church is the other side of the cloister through a second set of doors. This is a remarkable contrast since the interior is highly decorated in the Baroque style with a great deal of gilding, patterned marble, a number of large frescos and other paintings. The overall effect is much darker due to small high set windows and feels altogether heavier too, since although the architecture is regular and ordered, the intense level of decoration creates a very different impression from the cloister.

Nowhere is this more the case than around a very prominent votive chapel, itself quite unusual in that it is immediately to the left of the main entrance and built at the base of the nave. The chapel is in the form of a giant casket and not unlike a rather surreal outsized four-poster bed, with a huge sculpted canopy resting on four marble columns. The chapel houses a small altar and the surrounding structure has many candles on ornate holders as well as a number of chasubles for incense burning which are suspended on chains from the canopy's edge. There is an abundance of gold, brass and silver on display and all of it contributes to a scene that is laden with religious imagery.

Within this highly decorated area is the reason the altar is located in this unusual position. The priest stands within the chapel to celebrate mass and to pray before a painting of the annunciation which is situated on the back wall of the church. It is a simple fresco of Mary and the angel, about four feet high and rises above the altar. It has a rich gilded frame, is also now protected by glass and has a very dramatic large metal surround above it consisting of two angels in flight, supporting a central divine crown.

The tale is told that a monk started this piece one day in 1252, not long after the first church building on this site was completed, but unable to finish the face of the Madonna to his satisfaction he left his paints and brushes to one side to sleep. On waking he discovered a miracle had occurred, the painting had been completed by angels!

Both the cloister by Michelozzo and this 'miraculous Madonna' with all its attendant decoration are powerful examples of forms that hold a certain density of symbolism. For viewers there is a clear invitation to become participants in a particular experience which has been created by the artists and craftspeople who made these spaces.

Both experiences can take us beyond their most immediate details to other aspects which the visual arrangements and designs stand for. The Madonna connects with the world of the spirit and with the Christian belief in angelic realms, whereas Michelozzo reinvents traditions of Greek and Roman architecture to express ideas of beauty and the relationship of man to a divine order. The work exists both as the presentation of the immediate forms and also as the presence of all that they either stand for, or draw in, by association.

It is the nature of symbolic forms that they present a certain paradox. It is a paradox in the sense that art and design very often involves the skilful creation of objects and images which are, to some degree, designed to be a number of experiences at the same time. No one would be surprised that such symbolism is used to take the viewer beyond the everyday and to reach out to metaphysical experience; art has a long tradition of such use in a religious context. However, this does not only relate to work representing traditions of belief, in fact it is a phenomena that is seen in all art and design at an absolutely fundamental level.

To illustrate how this comes about we can consider an object which on the face of it, may appear to be a very long way from this type of imagery. The Alessi lemon squeezer is a simple functional object but it is also very distinctive; it is a key work by Philippe Starck (b. 1949) from 1990 and is considered by some to be a modern classic of industrial design. The shape consists of three thin gently curving legs connected to a raised central core which is the squeezer; the centrepiece is symmetrical, ridged and takes the form of an inverted droplet with the rounded end at the top and the point at the base. To operate the squeezer a half lemon is turned on the top and the juice and the pips one presumes, drip down the ridges to the point and into any small cup or jug placed between the three legs beneath. This basic idea could have been produced in various ways and it would still function much the same. However what makes this a satisfying and imaginative piece is the way in which it gathers up a variety of symbolic associations through the design. This symbolism invites the viewer to make certain connections.

The most obvious association is that of 1950's and 60's space rockets and satellites and also by extension, American car design of that era. It looks a little like an elongated Soviet Sputnik with its central shape and extending prongs, whilst the symmetrical ridges also recall the futuristic tail light fins of the Cadillac cars of that era. If this object was scaled up it would also be easy to see it playing a part in a science fiction B movie.

It is a solid piece of cast aluminium and it shines in a hard alien way. The tripod legs accentuate this quality further as they rise to a stylised angular corner before travelling inwards to join the body of the squeezer. The striding form also connects strongly with the invading tripods from H.G. Wells 'War of the

Worlds'. It is certainly not a welcoming shape; rather it has a quite aggressive quality.

The hard mechanical associations link neatly with the psychology of space rocket design too, where the power and toughness of a metal case protects the vulnerability of the cosmonauts. The difference here though is that the alien tripod exists not to protect but to scoop out and destroy the soft lemon, its juice will be removed and the skin discarded. It seems that in the kitchen there will be many lemons and only one victorious metal squeezer. It is not even an easy size and shape to put away so one suspects it will be on display standing tall on a kitchen surface, perpetually threatening the contents of the fruit bowl.

The function of squeezing lemons is common to many devices, but only Starck's design connects this function to the symbols of the space race and science fiction fantasy. The nature of the paradox is that these associations are both there and 'not there'; the object is a simple metal form with a job to do, but also stands for other aspects of the world which whilst both elsewhere and of a different time, are now present in a new way. The squeezer and the Madonna both rely on our ability to relate to and use symbols in this way.

As far as we know we are unique as a species in that we use this type of symbolic communication, and artists and designers often capitalise on the creative potential of symbolism in their work. Artists' processes have to engage with these symbolic dimensions too, as these qualities are not something at which a creative individual suddenly arrives; rather it is usually part of the gradual transformation and development of work.

The root of the capacity we have to share and to communicate using symbols comes from the very early stages of human development and involves the point at which a small child first becomes aware that there is a world beyond itself. The mismatch between a small baby's appetites and desires and the responses of the world (usually focussed on the relationship with the mother) creates the primary experience that the world is not simply within the mind of the child, but actually has an external quality and contains 'others'.

The infant's wilful cries attract responses and over a period of time they become the basis on which language starts to be formed. Rudimentary spoken works are the very start of the use of symbols to interact with the world. For example, 'Da Da' is the sound the child makes; it is not the father, but the child knows that it stands for the collection of 'otherness' which is the father. In order for this to be so, the child has had to reach a point where there is an internalised mental image of the father to which the noise is associated as a symbol. Also, the sound is already a shared symbol which others around have passed onto to the child through this process of learning.

From this type of beginning, we move forward into a world where we continually learn to build meaning in terms of symbolic experience.

The best way of defining a symbol for the purposes of exploring artistic creativity is that it simply stands for 'otherness to which we have a relationship'. From this standpoint it also becomes possible to understand a little more about the way in which ideas are generated. In order to create, artists need to have an active connection to the fundamental 'otherness' of the world as they look, draw, collect, record and photograph to investigate this relationship; they are continually engaging with varying types of symbolic activity by encountering the world in this way as they work.

We are accustomed to the phrase 'artistic statement' being applied to completed artwork, perhaps often for work in a fine art context. However it also clearly applies to functional designs such as stylised kitchen implements or magazine page spreads if they are lifted beyond ordinary workaday qualities by their creators. These can also be symbolic statements and just as 'Da Da' is the noise symbolising the father, so the artwork presents and communicates symbolic aspects of the relationship the artist experiences to a complex world.

Of course there is a much richer level of sophistication in the work of a mature artist, but the capacity to communicate using symbols remains essentially the same. The artist also explores through playing with this capacity; to test out and to seek to reconfigure new possibilities is an essential part of the artist's creative activity. This reinvention is part of the process of refreshing a relationship to the world; artists deliberately change the context of symbols and experience, often by putting unexpected things together to create new and exciting forms.

The lemon squeezer is a fine illustration of this process.

Choose a piece of artwork which you enjoy but mystifies or intrigues you in some way. Carry out an exercise where you think through the deconstruction of its symbolic content. This is not a wholly analytic task, but an imaginative one; ask yourself how does this work lead me to experience the 'otherness' of the world? How does it connect? What does it associate to and draw into the experience in order to communicate as a creative object? This approach could be applied to a number of pieces of work that have personal significance for you.

A further step could be to apply this type of thinking to your own work. If all art making involves activating a symbolic relationship to the world in some way, then how is this true in the case of your own work?

A word of caution though, this type of analysis can be fascinating and revealing, however, it is important to conduct it with a certain 'lightness of touch'. The risk is that any approach which is too heavy and especially over intellectualised, can paradoxically start to blind an artist or viewer to the actual content and potential of the work. This is sometimes the curse of curators and critics where the language used can disconnect from the work and a journey into types of 'art theory' can start to become a separate activity.

If you are conducting this type of reflective work for yourself, try to keep the relationship between the thoughts, notes and the work, quite open. A great principle is to ask a variety of questions about possible links, but not actually provide any definitive answers!

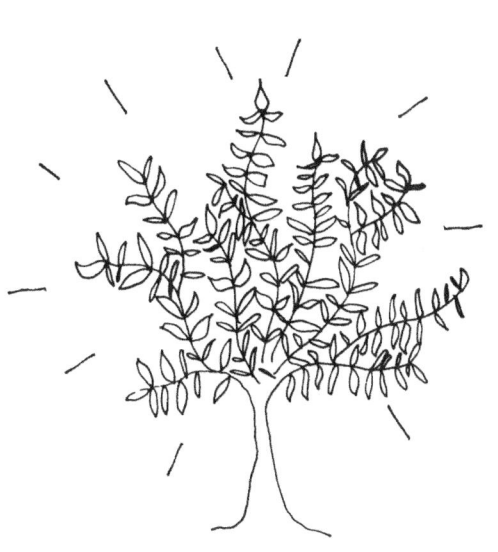

To be Original

Developing creativity is a very personal experience. Whether or not we know that similar ideas have been explored before and it is quite likely they have, we feel that the work belongs to us and is a product of our own effort and initiative. As we create art, we are usually seeking to somehow bring a unique sensibility to the activity, and to some degree we hope that there will be a spirit of originality in the work.

However, being original is not the same as having a personal quality. Originality is best understood socially and culturally since no individual artist can simply announce that their own work is original and it becomes so. It may well feel strongly personal to the artist but originality is about how the work finds its place in the world; it is how art work is received and understood by communities and the wider culture that is the marker of originality.

The psychoanalyst and writer Donald Winnicott describes culture as 'the common pool of humanity, into which individuals and groups of people may contribute, and from which we all may draw if we have somewhere to put what we find'[12]. Within this common pool of humanity, which forms culture in its broad-

12 Winnicott, Playing and Reality, p. 99.

est sense, there are many distinct areas of creative activity such as the visual arts, theatre, architecture, poetry, product design, music and dance. These are often linked with other cultural traditions, for example political theatre and religious architecture. Such relationships form an important part of our daily lives, creating complex networks of interrelated social and cultural experience. A common metaphor used is that of cultural and social 'fabric', as if our contact with these interwoven cultural fields has an almost physical nature. The work we make as artists becomes cultural as it finds its way into this fabric.

Much work that may not be highly original will find a place in this way; however there is a very important tension between creative work and the existing culture. This is the tension between what already exists and the 'newness' that we as artists can create; it is the relationship between 'tradition and originality'. Culture needs to be refreshed, changed and moved forward in order to be a living culture and this is a key role which artists and creative individuals frequently take on.

Winnicott states that 'in any cultural field it is not possible to be original except on a basis of tradition'[13]. Originality, whether it is radical and revolutionary, or subtle and delightful, is always born from a 'refiguring' of that which came before. This is why artists both enjoy and make reference to the work of others. Seeing other good art and design inspires and fuels our own imagination, as we see the phenomenal variety which has been achieved by others. The traditions we experience help to move our own work forward and if we are fortunate, they are the basis upon which to discover our own originality.

---

13 Winnicott, Playing and Reality, p. 99.

To achieve a productive balance between both tradition and an original approach is not a straightforward task for artists; the British sculptor Leonard McComb said 'in art it is easy to be personal; the real problem is to speak to strangers'[14]. To do this artists explore a shared visual culture as they work, and it is the response to what is shared which enables communication to occur.

Sometimes we may think that that originality is an exclusive and rare quality, only for the most highly gifted, but this is not so. If this were the case few would be involved in the creative arts and yet many are. We are all creating work within existing traditions, but equally we seek to add something new if we can. If we have nothing to contribute, if we have no energy, no fresh-ness, no new idea to try, no personal sensibility to explore and develop in the work, then all we can hope for is pastiche, weak copying or re-presenting of what already is. This type of work is fairly easy to find and superficially it may look like creative work, but it is not. The farthest end of the spectrum might be the heavily textured impressionist landscape paintings which can be purchased in some department stores and originate from factories in the far east. This work has the appearance of art based on a part of the western tradition, but it is a very long way from the raw and exciting revolution which occurred during the Impressionist era. The canvases look like art but they are not. Whilst this is an extreme example it serves to illustrate the risk of superficial art making which exists for us all. When working within a tradition, whether it is typographic design, abstract painting, photography, whatever, it is easy to be derivative, to

---

14 McComb, Exhibition Catalogue, p. 66.

rely too heavily on the style and the approach of others. If we do this it can certainly have the appearance of creative work, but there will be an important 'something' missing. This vital component is not an exclusive rarity; it is open to any that choose to seek it.

The chances of achieving a sense of originality and authenticity are raised by maintaining an energetic and questioning engagement with the work and the world. By exploring and testing out responses to the visual and wider culture, by not taking things for granted and working to try to really see things for ourselves in a fresh way, it becomes much more likely that we can make forms which communicate a sense of lively connection and invention to others.

Unsurprisingly this requires both time and work, but the process is highly rewarding and satisfying. If we consider originality to be the way in which we give new things an identity and a presence in the world for the very first time, then this is very motivating. We can create things in the world that have never existed before, similar perhaps, but never quite as we have made them. In this way we help keep traditions and culture alive.

It can sometimes appear that artists have done everything we could imagine or wish for. Wherever our enthusiasms lay we can find things we like, we only have to start to look. For artists the cultural pool of which Winnicott speaks is exceptionally deep. We dip into this pool and experience creative aspects of our culture which enrich and inform our own visual imagination.

We can see the work of artists and designers in our everyday surroundings, as well as when we visit exhibitions. As we investigate the work of other artists and cultures relevant to our developing ideas interests and needs, it is worth remembering that we usually share some important common ground with many other artists even if they work quite differently. We might view artistic expression as an artist somehow communicating an important part of their experience of living. It is almost as if they are giving form to the statement 'this is what it is like to be alive, to be me in the world'. Viewed in this way, work by other artists can be like a voice of a companion calling, to aid us in our own task; this power of communication can often seem to transcend some of the barriers of time and cultural difference. This is a source of richness and inspiration, without which our own creativity would dwindle to nothing, since artists do not only nourish culture generally, they also 'feed' each other.

A primary way in which artists are connected to culture is through participation in communities; this is how we both contribute to the wider world and also how we learn and grow as artists. Some communities are formally organised to support this, for example within classes at a college, or work place groups, or through less formal associations of artists and designers who may collaborate for particular projects. Other connections are less definite but also very important; for example we may network and strike up conversations and contacts with others enabling us to share and develop ideas.

There are times when work can be extremely collaborative and team orientated; big projects of many types require this, but creative activity also requires moments of solitude and singular thought. There is an interesting tension between the social aspects of art making which absolutely depend on communities, and the separation from these experiences which creative work also requires. The latter may be through concentrated time in a studio, or with work spread out on a bedroom floor, perhaps whilst sketching ideas in a drawing book on a long train journey. It is absolutely clear that solitude in thought and production is required as ideas are processed, developed and turned over in the mind. The Romantic notion of a 'solitary' genius can start to figure here; however this idea can be quite misleading as it is one amplified by popular myth rather than wholly based in reality. Even those artists held to have a unique spark of individual vision do not achieve this without their communities. For example, Van Gogh fits the mould of an isolated visionary, misunderstood and unappreciated by his contemporaries, unsuccessful as an artist in his own lifetime and therefore quite alone. This is the myth; however, his letters reveal him as someone who always drew inspiration from the people around him. He was deeply committed to social activity and was greatly influenced by the creative work of his contemporaries, as well as the art of the past.

Another figure who looms large in the popular imagination for different reasons, but to similar effect, is Michelangelo. He is viewed as an 'heroic' genius, single-handedly painting the majestic Sistine Chapel ceiling, and creating the David as a celebration of his unique artistic power and vision from a giant block of solid marble. Both these instances tell us something of the strength of individual vision, but the popular view underestimates the enormous power of community which underpins all artistic activity and this is especially so in these examples. All artists need good teachers (Michelangelo was no exception) since we have to learn from others at every stage of our lives. Great artists are not born great, they have to grow and find a place in the world, and there are many examples where artistic achievement is impossible without a fulsome commitment from large numbers of creative individuals working together. The field of architecture is possibly the clearest example of this in the visual arts, but even a single great painting or sculpture is impossible to achieve without community; indeed the very notion of 'original work' exists as a social experience. There are many things in life which cannot be achieved alone and achieving a measure of originality within the visual arts is certainly one such activity.

Create a visual map of your own artistic heritage. Place a suitable symbol in the centre to represent yourself then start to add in markers to show your influences e.g. teachers, colleagues, fellow artists, key moments of influence and change, places you have visited that have made an impact and particularly significant pieces of artwork. As you add these things, place them in relation to yourself to show their relative importance. Use scale, colour and position to visualise connections.

Start a collaborative project; involve a musician, a dancer or a writer in a visual arts show. Explore how the flow of ideas across disciplines might enrich a presentation of the work.

Create some art which crosses cultural fields;
 Make a sculpture which celebrates a piece of music.
 Make a painting about a poem.
 Produce a graphic image that illustrates a dance style.
 Design a typeface which celebrates an event.

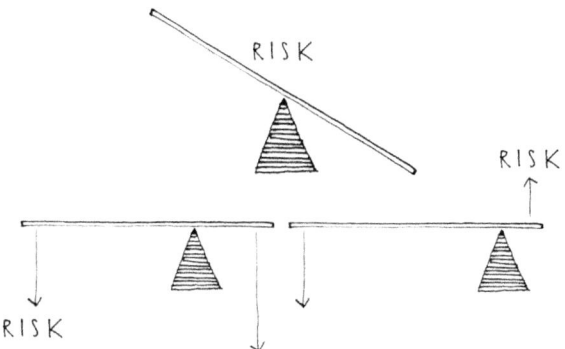

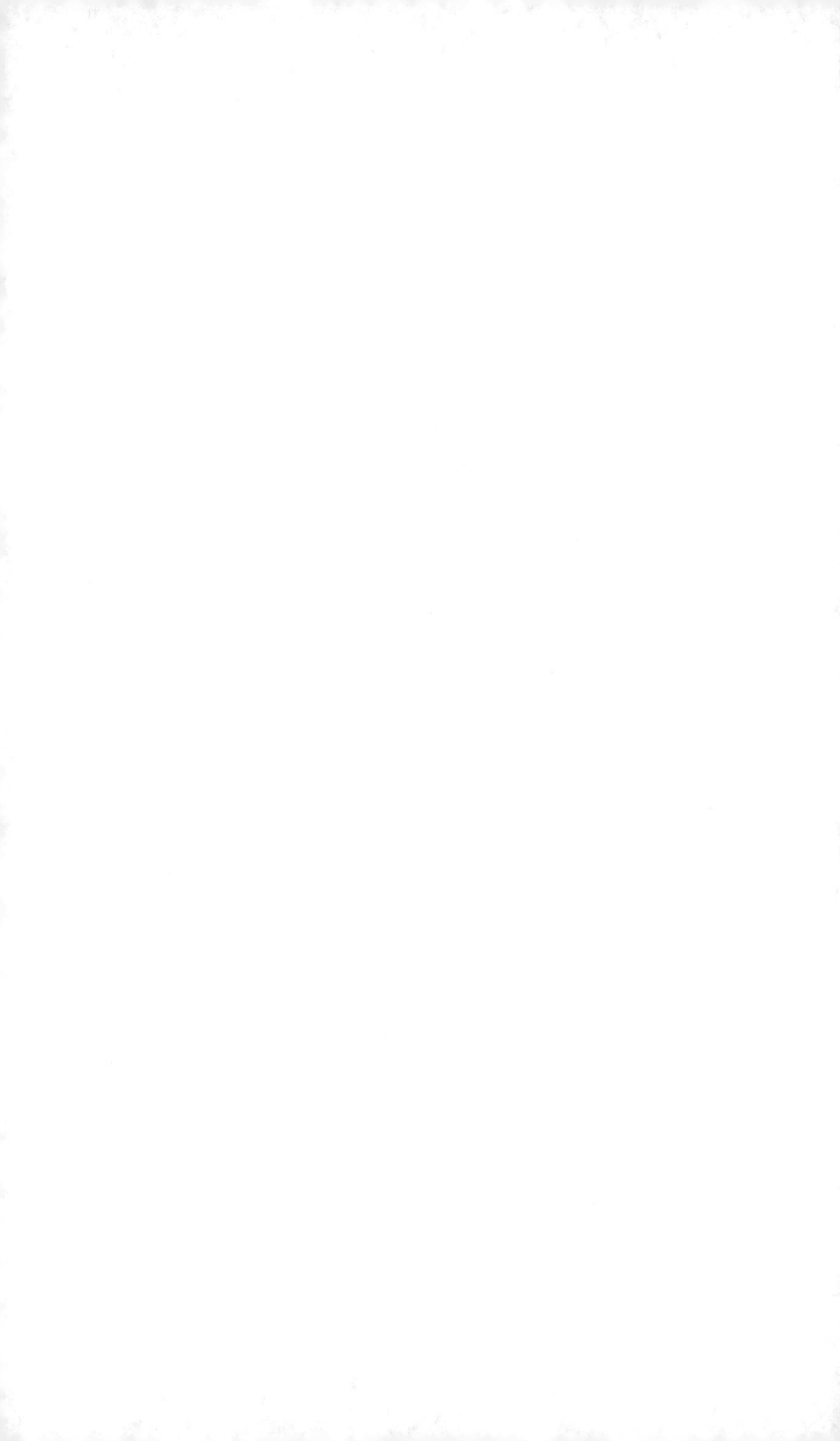

INTELLECT, INTUITION AND RISK

The relationship between an artist's intellect and what we usually call intuition is at the heart of developing creative work. Creativity often involves achieving a balance between these sometimes-contradictory aspects of our minds. This can also be described as the difference between thinking and feeling, and both of these capacities have a bearing on that most important step in the creative process which involves 'taking a risk'.

Our intellect is concerned with that which can be thought, spoken, analysed, discussed. In art making the intellect supports our conscious planning and thoughtful anticipation, an intention for an image and ideas we can share in discussion as we work. Intuition, however, is connected to a more emotional quality of experience; phrases that we often use when we talk about intuition include having 'a hunch' or going by 'gut feeling'. We simply say that something 'feels' right without needing to back it up with a spoken justification. Sometimes to talk too much risks spoiling or losing the energy behind a hunch; we simply need to follow our intuition and make things.

When working with images, success often means the intellectual side of our mind needs to be relaxed. We might have a host of intentions and ideas, but paradoxically the best way of realising them might be to forget them, at least during certain phases of our making. It is something that all artists recognise. We can become lost in the process, we forget time and enter a state where it seems we 'forget ourselves'. It is not that we stop thinking; it is more that we set aside the rational and analytic part of our mind and work in a way that moves ahead of our thinking. The artist Alex Katz suggests 'paint faster than you can think'[15].

In the Western tradition we might consider this as the interplay between consciousness and the boundary of our unconscious mind, with its complex patterning of emotion, instincts and memory. It is by definition a resource that is not accessible by purely conscious recall. In the Eastern tradition, Zen masters might call this 'big mind' whereby the small mind of the individual self is put aside, and we connect with greater resources and more universal and mysterious aspects of our humanity. Regardless of how we might conceptualise what is happening as we work intuitively, it is clear that the experience feels quite different from producing a pre-prepared plan. Spontaneity, improvisation and a different type of relaxed reflection come to the fore. Often the work can become much stronger during this phase; the 'unexpected' can more easily enter the process, and often the unexpected seems to fit well with our intentions. This is not co-incidental.

In 1967 the artist and teacher Anton Ehrenzweig[16] wrote extensively about the relationship between this intuitive state and its relationship to the intellect. He describes this as a cyclical process; that is to say after becoming 'one with our work'

---

15 Fischl and Saltz, Sketchbook with Voices, p. 38

16 Ehrenzweig, The Hidden Order of Art.

when we become lost in the experience of making, we have to become separate again. We need to bring our intellectual and analytic conscious mind back to the activity. Sometimes this can be uncomfortable and artists know this experience only too well. We talk of seeing things 'in the cold light of day' perhaps away from the passion and involvement we had felt. We recognise what it is to return to artwork and be disappointed that it is not as good as we had previously felt. This is due to our changing, not the work changing; our mind is simply behaving differently.

If this is the case, Ehrenzweig proposes that we should continue with the work, and allow ourselves to go back into the 'cycle' of creation which involves the interplay of intellect and intuition; two kinds of 'mind'.

The ease with which people can work intuitively seems to vary for different individuals and to a degree it seems linked to personal disposition. These qualities do seem to shape individual characteristics, as people tend to have personal attributes that can lean towards different ends of a spectrum. This has been recognised for a long time. For example, there is a strong connection between the intellect and intuition and the principles once described by the Greeks as the Apollonian spirit of cool rational ideas and order and the Dionysian spirit of passion, poetry and chaos. Artists need to work with both capacities, but as they too are often weighted in a particular direction, it is sometimes difficult to achieve a productive interplay between these two key qualities. This is highlighted when a problem is being worked with and there is an intention or set of ideas which is being explored, and yet the work is going badly. The results are awkward and unsatisfactory and no matter what is tried, nothing seems to improve the work or carry it forward in a good way; frustration sets in. At this point we feel defeated and sometimes, almost in desperation, we might do a few things to the work which feel initially like destructive gestures. We might dismantle or reconfigure something quickly, or draw over a crafted design roughly. I think it is important to give in to this feeling of defeat, wholly, and yet to continue to work. What can happen is that intuition can really take over at this point. It might feel that we have abandoned our conscious planned approach totally, but actually we may be just relaxed enough to allow a new way of working to come to the fore. A different part of our mind takes the lead. Using these moments well is one of the highest creative skills since it requires a quality of openness and watchfulness to spot the opportunities in the work at this point. The notion of rebirth, that good things can come out of what appears to be disaster, or a phoenix rising from ashes, is a good way to consider the possibilities of these moments.

There are ways in which artists can choose to promote more intuitive ways of working right from the start of developing ideas; this is through the deliberate use of 'risk'. Given that we work with materials which may be unpredictable, and that the intellectual grip on our activity is often relaxed as we give way to the power of intuition, it is no surprise that as artists we value risk.

Risk is at the heart of what we do to create images which are new to us. The risk we take is that of failure and we all have in-built resistance to failure, or at least a desire not to be seen to fail, so to take risks does require a certain amount of confidence.

There is an established tradition in Western art education where the teaching of risk-taking is viewed as an essential part

104

of the induction of art and design students. Linked to a fear of failure, young artists (and old ones too) may be limited and constrained by habitual ways of working. They may view their work as too precious, too much the result of a struggle, or time, or skill, to be genuinely open to risk; if mistakes occur they could result in the destruction of what has been achieved.

To help develop confidence in risk taking, a whole range of methods may be applied; such as drawing with the 'wrong' hand, drawing blind, making a sudden radical change of scale, or attaching a drawing tool to the end of a long stick to disrupt the usual processes of control with mark-making. Students at the Bartlett School of Architecture are sent out on a walk to find a random discarded object in the streets, and then directed to base a design project on this selection. These are examples of ways in which habits are challenged; chance is deliberately used to disrupt the expected and the attitude to experimentation and risk-taking is fostered.

If we only ever attempted the things we knew we could do we would never make discoveries, and we would never surprise ourselves. The artist Benny Andrews suggests 'keep yourself off balance because the process allows for a certain amount of discovery'[17]. In practice this means resisting the desire to repeat a past success and maybe selecting a different material or process to take an idea in an uncertain direction.

Closely allied to risk is an experimental attitude. We can enjoy not knowing quite what will happen with a particular piece or project, and yet at the same time we play with our growing strengths and enthusiasms. Andrews advises keeping

---

17 Fischl and Saltz, Sketchbook with Voices, p. 42

off balance as we need to move between what we can do and what we might do.

There is a definite relationship between the use of risk and intuition. It is possible to work in a 'risky' way for a prolonged period and to say to oneself 'I am simply trying out some things', no pressure, no blame, no judgement and perhaps only a light guiding conscious intention. The pile of unresolved work might get quite big, but this is fine. It is possible to simply allow the unexpected in, as this type of process develops its own momentum; one image leads to another and by allowing any anxiety about failure to slip away, a lighter more free method can take over. This is rather like free word association or jazz improvisation; it involves quick uncluttered responses which can often fit in surprising ways as we create experiences and forms which we would not necessarily expect.

In this phase of creativity it is important to value everything, especially things that initially look least acceptable. I have observed many occasions both in my work and the work of students when, after a little time has elapsed, sometimes the most disliked result can actually be a key to developing something new and unexpected. This is a little like the principle that reflection on why one may strongly dislike certain people can reveal something interesting about us, rather than the disliked individual. Nothing is an error or an irritant or a failure in this type of experimental attitude to work; everything is potentially an unexpected 'gift', so being slow to judge and watchful are useful qualities to foster.

The ability to take risks is an essential part of allowing creativity to function, since without risk nothing new can happen.

Think of the moments when you have been 'lost' in the process of making, when any fixed ideas about what you thought you might achieve seem to evaporate, but something better happened. What are the conditions that seem to promote these moments for you? What are the conditions that stop this from happening?

Draw an image with the hand you would not normally use. The principle of disruption should never be far away when working creatively; if you can create the conditions of instability, surprise is more likely.

Find a piece of work which has good shapes and arrangement but is not finished - pour a quantity of ink onto it from a height - try to rescue it by wiping some off - let it dry and continue to complete it in a new way which works with the residue of the accidental marks created by the ink.

Make a big shared drawing with a partner, use black and white chalks - have no ideas or theme beyond trying to fill the page in an interesting way - occasionally turn the page so you both work on the full page - negotiate the finish.

Show a piece of your work to someone whose opinion you value and ask for their thoughts. Select someone who would not normally see your work.

Plan some rules that involve throwing a dice to determine the course of a piece of work, e.g. throw every minute, a six equals straight lines only, until an odd number is thrown. Experiment with chance rules and the impact of these on a development process;

see the Chance and Order series of paintings and drawings by Kenneth Martin (1905-1984) for some examples.

Be light-hearted with drawing – what is the smallest drawing you can make? Make a series of drawings on paper from a hole-punch machine, create accompanying notes and curate a miniature drawing exhibition.

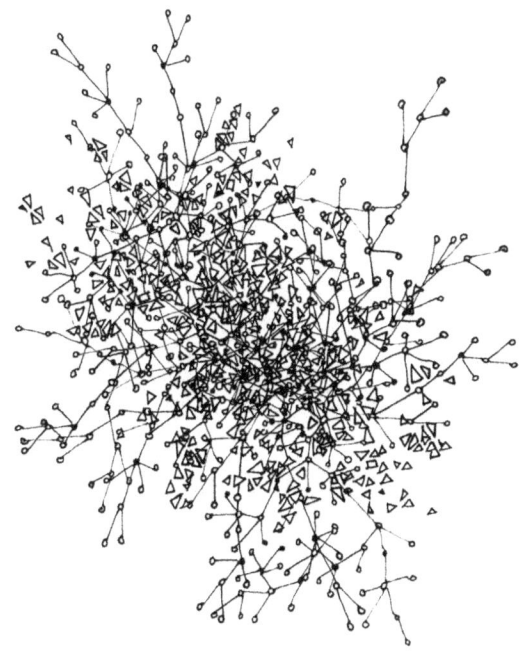

Imagination and Inspiration

Imagination is the ability to see a range of possibilities and then to bring the best of these possibilities into being in some way. It is both a power of the mind and of action in the world, and as such it is never abstract and unreal. Imagination is also closely linked with the notion of inspiration since seeing possibilities is not a neutral capacity; it is linked to desire and a passionate connection to the world. As artists our ability to imagine is continually fed by special encounters with the world, and also by the work and example of other creative individuals.

We can consider the specific nature of artistic imagination and how it supports creativity by starting from what is commonly said about imagination. For example, if we say 'that's a very imaginative solution', an artist may have visualised possibilities in order to arrive at a solution to a problem. Also 'imagine yourself in my position' is an appeal to think and feel as another might about a situation. Both these statements describe transformations that are driven by the mind. Viewed in this way, imagination allows us to hold possibilities in our mind, to create and consider a mental image of them and to understand and feel the potential quality of this transformation, without initially having to actually change anything.

111

We know that imaginative people are those who seem to be able to see and think further ahead than others; their achievements are sometimes totally unexpected but seem to feel absolutely right. We sometimes say that they have 'vision'; they hold within them thoughts and feelings of how things might be different and they have the will and influence to move towards this, often taking others with them as they share this imaginative vision. We value this highly and it is a quality that great artists have in common with great leaders.

Sometimes people say 'it is from my imagination', but I do not believe that the imagination is a mental 'place' to get things from. This can be an unproductive idea for artists because it views the world as a real external fact and our minds as separate unreal internal worlds. Here imagination is inside our minds and therefore not real. As creative artists it is more useful to view the imagination as a real process rather than an unreal place.

The 20th century French philosopher Gaston Bachelard described the imagination as a highly creative process, which is not concerned with merely mentally reproducing an external world. He says 'the imagination is not a faculty which fabricates images of [external] reality; it is a power which forms images which surpass reality in order to change reality'[18].

This is creative imagination! This is imagination that holds and considers a range of possibilities and then allows us to move ahead to bring about the actual transformations, which give form and reality to these possibilities.

This is why imagination is so important to artists. We need to explore possibilities continually as we work, yet we have

18 Bachelard, On Poetic Imagination and Reverie, p. 93.

neither the time nor resources to create every possible image. Imagination is the power to visualise as yet unrealised possibilities as we work. In this way we can be very efficient workers; when work is going well, acceptance and rejection of these imagined possibilities can happen at a furious rate.

However, imagination is rarely straightforward, particularly as it seems to have an ability to pull artists in two directions simultaneously. As we work with materials, we need to imagine them reconfigured and arranged into a new state, a new settled design. But at the same time, to be able to do this, we are continually undoing and imaginatively unmaking in order to have the flexibility we need to move images forward. Imagination pulls us towards completion and rest, but also to creative fragmentation and unrest. It is no wonder artists occasionally have trouble knowing clearly if something is finished or not.

Imagination also has a curious spontaneity to its operations. For example, artists may often find that possible solutions to problems seemingly fly into their heads when they least expect, for example whilst showering, or when riding a bicycle, or last thing at night as sleep gradually takes hold. There is no doubt that the human mind has the ability to function differently when it is in a relaxed state and off duty. These are times during which I have found some of my own most engaging imaginative ideas come forward into consciousness.

Imagination can also be developed as a power, rather like other human capacities. Imaginative thinking involves rejecting the obvious and considering possibilities which might seem initially eccentric and out of step with what might be expected. It can be quite difficult to learn this approach as at a certain level it can sometimes feel 'wrong'. However this type of thinking can become embedded with practice. The science of brain research has shown how new links (neural pathways), actually grow in the brain as learning occurs, and so imaginative thinkers benefit from new pathways and connections which strengthen their ability to think in this way. The more we put our imagination to work, the quicker and stronger it becomes.

A powerful way to promote the activity of imagination can occur through deliberately encouraging a more 'full' relationship with an image as it evolves. To explore this, let me return to the idea that we are using cycles of thought and feeling, and of intellect and intuition to move our work forward; we are involved in a complex relationship between the work and ourselves. We also know that whilst working creatively we can experience a wide range of emotions when our involvement is high; joy and satisfaction, disappointment and frustration, clarity or confusion.

A key question is where else in our lives do we feel this variety of emotion and involvement? The answer is in our relationships with our significant others, with family, partners, children and close friends. Artists experience a variety of powerful feelings about artwork in a similar way. The reason for this is that we can all put feelings into relationships with objects, rather than people, quite easily. Consider how a small child feels about a special teddy, or an adult about a cherished object, be it a family heirloom or a new car. It is not as simple as having a feeling about an object; with certain things the feeling seems projected into the object and the object seems to contain and embody the feeling in some way.

When we are making art, something special happens with this common ability to project feelings. We use the projection of emotional experience to open out an 'imaginative space' that exists between the art object and us. This is a psychological space where we can experience not simply an emotion, but potentially a complex developing relationship with the art 'object' we make.

Winnicott described this phenomenon as a 'transitional space'[19], a transition between the fundamental otherness of the world and the experience of 'ourselves'. The 'transitional space' is clearly not in the physical art object we make, but neither is it inside us, somehow it is a blend.

This is a really useful idea for thinking about imagination because it is always active within this space, shaping, changing and shifting our experience of the world. This is the space from which new possibilities arise as we work.

In the transitional space, we experience a dialogue with the image we make. Because of what can happen as we work, we have to be watchful for the unexpected, and in a sense we have to listen to what our work has to say to us. We can achieve this by giving due regard to the independence of the work as it develops, and to be alive to the needs of the experience of 'otherness' which is taking shape before us. Ehrenzweig summarised this, stating that 'something like a true conversation takes place between an artist and his [or her] own work'[20]. This is not implying that we talk out loud to our work; the emphasis is on the idea of a dialogue that develops as we work and a true, authentic relationship where we give of our very best in the activity of making and we respond to the work as it is created.

To give of one's best in this way is a continual challenge. There is a well known saying that creative work is '99% per-

---

19 Winnicott, Playing and Reality.

20 Ehrenzweig, The Hidden Order of Art, p. 57.

spiration and 1% inspiration' and it would certainly seem true that the energy going into the relationship comes largely from within. However, inspiration is a vital part of the dynamics existing between the artist and the work. Inspiration usually refers to how energy and ideas come from elsewhere to shape this relationship. I think that 1% may be rather low, if indeed this could ever be measured.

When we say we have been inspired, we usually mean that we have made a connection with something in the world; it might well be the work of other artists, but it may be a particular experience, for example visiting a special place, or having a motivating conversation. This connection then has the ability to energise creative activity. The word 'inspiration' comes from the same root as respiration and it means 'to bring in breath or spirit'. For artists, being inspired describes the way in which the life and meaning of our work increases, and it is this process which energises the imaginative connection between the world and the work.

Artists actively seek these experiences, where the new floods in and connects with where we are. Sometimes this is a great challenge and inspiration can shake our certainties and preconceptions. In the best moments, something seems to 'click', to fit with what we intuitively hope for but cannot yet quite know. Whilst artists seek these experiences, we cannot exactly know what we seek until we find it, since inspiration involves a sense of 'otherness' and difference. Being inspired challenges us to become more than we are; this occurs through the interaction with things that are new to us.

Looking back on experiences which have inspired me and through discussing these with other artists, I see an interesting parallel between being inspired and falling in love. In many respects the highly significant moments of inspiration which occur as we develop as artists seem as much the experience choosing us, as our choosing the experience. In life you cannot help whom you fall in love with, it just happens and there are far too many variables to pin down exact reasons; inspiration also has this rich and unpredictable quality.

Inspiration and imagination are closely linked; when we encounter work which truly inspires us the experience causes our imaginative processes to become more and more active. We start to imagine the impact of new experiences on current or past ideas and new possibilities start to fluctuate before our mind's eye. We then need to act to test out and explore the implications of the inspiration.

Sometimes, the cycle of inspiration to action is relatively immediate; however, I am aware of artists for whom the formative nature of inspiration is so significant that sometimes the impact of these occasions can take years or even decades to explore. This can be so powerful that the experience can even alter the usual linear experience of time. Key moments of inspiration can become rather like a continual presence to which new experiences are brought to further articulate and explore this relationship.

All this is positive, but what about the problem of lack of imagination or inspiration? An imaginative world full of creative people could be seen as an impossible ideal. Much of the time imagination can seem to be absent as we live in a fairly mundane world, often full of fairly ordinary images and experiences. There are aspects of our world which can constrain imaginative work and also reduce the possibility of inspiration occurring.

117

Developed cultures run on a high density of images, for example, through advertising, entertainment and news media, politics and religion. Many of the images we experience may lack freshness and impact and there can often be considerable predictability; it is almost as if images get used up and worn out. The idea that images might wear out might seem a strange one, but by this I mean that we often encounter clichés and a certain emptiness in second or third-rate images. Sometimes this feels pleasant, since that with which we are familiar is often comfortable; however this is quite different from the new experiences and visions which artists, designers and other creative people present as culture is made new again.

Images get worn out in the wider culture with the energy and authenticity somehow gone, and it is a fact that this can also happen during the process of making artwork; this is particularly true when we feel lost or stuck with an image. Whilst in everyday life most of us can be at ease with the second rate for quite a lot of the time, it is clear that whilst making art this is something we choose to avoid; and yet sometimes this is how it goes. It is almost as if we wear out the images which we ourselves are trying to realise in a piece of work.

Images can lose, or even fail to achieve life whilst we work in any number of ways. This can occur through over familiarity and looking at them for too long, or by allowing materials to become overworked and tired. Sometimes we lose sight of an idea because it is too difficult and the habits of how we make and handle images take over. Somehow we create something which is weak and has lost contact with the quality of an image which we aspire to and imagine.

Wearing out an image in one of these ways is actually incredibly easy, and much of the best teaching a young artist receives is never simply about pure technical skill, but about how to keep the relationship with images fresh and alive. This is one reason why artists may deliberately use varieties of materials, technique and scale as they shift the dynamics of a developing image. These types of strategies are useful as they stop us grasping at images too tightly. If we find that our images are getting worn out, we need to be bold to refresh them to open out new possibilities in order to move forward. It is not simply the artwork that gets tired and weak, it may be that the imaginative space between us and the work has almost shut down and so we have to work to re-energise this relationship.

Think of an image by an artist who is really special to you, a favourite, one that really does the things you feel art should do, put the image in your journal. Record why it is special, note down when you first started to notice these things and how this has affected how you feel and think about art.

Work with a friend to come up with ideas for developing a new piece or theme. Work on a big sheet of paper with chunky felt pens, get really competitive and see if you can write down one hundred key words and ideas. Be bizarre, logical, vague, clear, and above all associate freely, speak and argue whilst doing it. Try to achieve the magic one hundred in ten minutes if you can. When complete, pin up the sheet. Review the connections and variations; reflect on the implications of the best ideas for your work.

The following suggestions should be undertaken as simple sketch-book tasks and can offer oblique, yet potentially revealing reflections, on the nature of the imaginative space that exists between us and our work[21].

Most tasks should be followed by the clause 'about your work', e.g.
   'confess your secrets… about your work':
write a manifesto
write a recipe for your creative process
write a diary entry
be interviewed by your own questions
confess your secrets
give fair warning
write an hypothesis
write a journalistic news item
tell a joke
give the viewer instructions
write a postcard
borrow someone else's voice
be ridiculous
define some categories
make an index of relevant words
be ironic
rant and rave
be hysterically paranoid
tell a lie
write a letter to your work – then write the reply
explain the difficulty of using words and how this is difficult in the

---

21 Jones, Artist Teacher Course lecture notes.

case of your work

write directions (or draw a map) showing how to get from A to B in
your work

conjure with the magic of your creativity

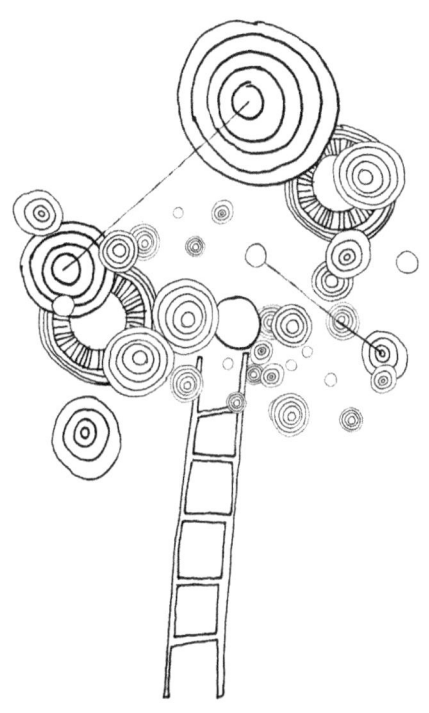

Dreaming and Daydreaming

To 'dream something up' is a revealing statement which relates to certain aspects of creativity. 'I just dreamt it up' can be a throwaway comment, or 'where did you dream that up from?' can express astonishment. Such language points to the appearance of the unpredictable and the unprecedented; it seems to have come from nowhere. But nothing comes from nowhere, and the relationship between dreaming, imagination and creative vision has a long and established history.

Dreaming during sleep is at the far end of a spectrum of imaginative life. We do not have to make any effort to have dreams which are imaginative and surprising, as they simply 'are', even though they are usually fairly random and nonsensical. The strange and arbitrary nature of dream images can be interpreted successfully on occasions to reveal meaning which may not be inaccessible in any other way. This is an ancient tradition linked both to prediction of future events and revelations of significant truth. There are celebrated examples of this such as Joseph's Old Testament dream of the fat and thin cattle warning of seven years of famine, and in recent times the scientist James Watson's dream of two intertwined snakes revealing the now famous interpretation of the structure of the DNA double helix.

The latter is particularly interesting since the dream world is usually considered to be at the opposite end of an imaginative spectrum to the natural sciences. The ideals of the Enlightenment gave birth to modern science through an enormous shift towards rational thought, logical analysis and the drive to identify, measure and quantify; by contrast, dreaming is chaotic, unpredictable, illogical and impossible to quantify. These latter qualities found a place in the hearts of the Romantic artists of the 19th century as they reacted against the dominance of the new rational order of the industrial age. The influence of the dream world in the minds of western artists can easily be traced from this time through the work of the Symbolists at the turn of the 20th century, to the chaos of Dada and into the explicit dream content of the Surrealists.

The tension between these two dominant themes in Western culture had a huge impact on creative developments across the whole of the last century. In art and design, the ideal of progress towards a better world through human ingenuity reached a zenith in the traditions of 20th century Modernism through ground breaking design and architecture. Set against this, after the initial rupture and reaction of Romanticism, many artists went on to delve deeper and deeper into the unpredictable world of dreams. Artistic connections were made to metaphysical symbolism, the occult and that least scientific branch of experimental psychology, psychoanalysis. From the 1920s to the 50s as Modernism hurtled towards the purity of antiseptic glass, metal, concrete and functional minimalism, many artists were often getting dirty in the chaos of the dream world. This is not to say that these approaches are polar opposites; the relationships are more complex than this. However, these two very different sets of ideas do seem to pull artists and designers in quite different directions.

It is possible to see a very distinct 'dreaming' dimension in the story of 20th century art up to the end of the 1950's. American Abstract Expressionism was the last major art movement to explore this directly; by the time Rothko and Pollock were its leading figures, their art was laying claim to mystic and transcendental qualities and proposing channels of connection through art to the most mysterious aspects of our existence.

To some extent the approach of these artists was in sympathy with the aims of Modernism. Although they proposed links to the spirirtual and the unfathomable, they did so with a heroic stance, and crucially with a sense that to travel deeper into this murkiness represented a type of radical progress. They led, so viewers and other artists might follow and connect with some of the most profound experiences that art could offer.

However, as the 1960s began, many of the cherished ideals of cultural progress through both science and art started to collapse. The post-war, post-nuclear age now shed a new and much harsher light on a very different kind of technological world. This became an era of great questioning and art was also involved in this appraisal. Artistic statements of mystery and deep meaning were out, and artists looked to the everyday world to create a fresh connection to their imagination through what became known as Pop Art.

Imaginative dreaming had not gone away, instead it became taken up with a new lightness of touch; the dark and quite heavy approach of the Surrealists and the grandiose pretensions of the Abstract Expressionists had been rejected by the new generation. Instead, a new playfulness was born as artists connected many disparate parts of the contemporary world to create new types of experience. The combining of things and ideas that do not usually belong together had, in the hands of the Surrealists, been an exploration of the hinterland of dreams and the unconscious. In the hands of the Pop artists this approach became mainstream and in its remixing of an established cultural order, Pop art reflected a world where the old ideas of progress were becoming more complex and perhaps even slipping away. The Post Modern era was evolving and the chaotic dimensions of experience were no longer the province of a few groups of experimental artists. Instead, paradox and contradiction were placed at the heart of a new popular culture; high art and low art became intertwined, and artists such as Rauschenburg and Rosenquist also made reference to contemporary technology with a new found ambiguity.

Although there have been many developments in art since the sixties, in the early 21st century we are still living in an epoch of questioning and contradiction. In many respects the pressures and upheavals of the globalisation of trade and culture have amplified the experiences of paradox and unexpected connection. The making of art and how modern populations are making use of it, seems to reflect this too. Visit any major contemporary art collection and it is possible to view art making and also art viewing, as a form of mass cultural dreaming. Visitors encounter work that often has no explicit function; this is not work which supports a particular religion as in the past, and it is rarely purely decorative, although much of it is good to look at. The work often does not present accurate representations of things in the world; instead people are attracted by the mystery of the work. The work is 'hard to understand' and of course this is partly the point of it. Like dreams, many of these works are visions which may reference many things we know, yet present us with experiences that are resistant to understanding and interpretation. The numbers viewing this type of work are very high too, suggesting that the appetite for this type of experience is great; in 2010 Britain's Tate Modern gallery was the second most visited London attraction after the British Museum, with over five million visits[22].

As artists work, they may not have a deliberate fascination with dream imagery and processes. However, it is within the experience commonly called daydreaming, that we all have a direct connection to much of the spontaneous and unpredictable qualities of imaginative and creative thinking. Often it seems artists do not have to try deliberately to imagine anything, since the mind conjures up images with a surprising independence, and sometimes images and ideas seem simply to appear and come to us rather like a dream. During sleep we have no control over what we dream, and whilst we are awake, ideas and solutions to problems can arise even when not actively thinking about our work. This is a little like remembering something you have forgotten but only after you stop trying to remember it; we say 'it will come to me' and sure enough it will. We know that our minds have resources and abilities that are well beyond the reach of wilful control.

There are times each day when we all experience the independent capacity of our waking minds to flow freely through the experience of daydreaming as we allow our minds to wander.

---

22 Bates, British tourist attraction visitor figures, Guardian Newspaper article (23/2/11)

The classic images of this are someone staring vacantly out of the window on a rainy day or into the flickering embers of a dying fire, but actually most people spend a great deal of time daydreaming without any special props at all. This occurs in the spaces between conversations and between all our more definite thoughts. As we go about our daily business our minds relax, thoughts wander, as we turn over a variety of possible memories and anticipations, often linked to places, times and situations, other than those in which we actually are. We do not choose the contents of this reverie, they simply appear. This experience is not the same as conscious thinking, it is broader and deeper, encompassing feelings, sequences and settings, all imagined and just out of range of wilful control. It is a fair assumption that for the majority of waking time we are never very far from this experience. During the last century, psychoanalysts explored how we are never fully asleep and analysed the meaning of our dreams, but crucially they also taught us that we are never fully awake. The independent dreaming capacity of our minds breaks into conscious thoughts and carries us away continually.

For the artist this is a special resource. We need to be continually watchful of what might turn up in the mind, not only during the times when we are making art, but also when we are away from our work. What new ideas, images, feelings and associations might fit well with or enrich some new work? We need to be especially watchful if we feel stuck, or unclear of how to move forward. Sometimes the next steps, a solution, or even a collection of ideas and images will come to our mind. It is as if our 'big mind' or dreaming mind has been working for us in another place away from our other more immediate activities. Actively creating a record of personal dreams is a way of developing and strengthening this capacity which may be useful for some; it can give the dreaming mind more of a presence in the waking day.

The key to using this imaginative dreaming capacity in our work more fully, is to develop an attitude of relaxed, yet acute, watchfulness. Like many things worth doing it does take practise. Sometimes images will be faint so try to follow them in your mind. Dream daydreams further and commit them as soon as you can to a real handmade image, even if it is just a quick sketch and a note. In this way they will achieve resonance, presence and meaning. Such images can grow and feed bigger tasks, often in unexpected ways, since they can be connected to rich creative resources within the mind.

Start a dream book, keep it by your bed and write down your dream immediately as you wake, so it does not slip away. It gets better with practise; if you like you can 'ask for a dream', out loud before you go to sleep; this might sound a little fanciful, but it really can dramatically increase the chance of having a dream you remember. Start to pick images from the dream book to work with. Choose ones which you feel you can develop and take further as you work; treat this as a process not an illustration.

Find an image from art history which looks like a scene from a story, make a drawing from it which plays with 'what might happen next'. Use the idea of imagining that you have dreamt the image, so your new drawing is like dreaming a little longer.

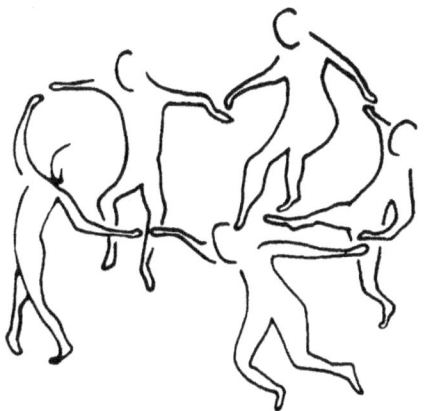

COMMUNICATION AND BEING

There is a long tradition that creativity has a relationship with psychological dimensions within the personality of the artist. For example, in the medieval era all personality types were thought to be the result of the 'four humours', and melancholia was the one ascribed to artists. This was believed to be caused by an unusually high amount of 'black bile' and was considered the least desirable disposition; it was also linked to insanity. Renaissance philosophers later looked a little more favourably on this; the dark brooding self-reflection and introversion of the melancholic artist was seen as a necessary dimension of the process of giving birth to new ideas and visions.

In the modern era, creativity has also been linked to depression, neurosis and compulsion, and the drive to create has often been depicted as having difficult dimensions which can strain personal relations. In extremis this can become deeply destructive for the individuals concerned. Tales of famously 'tortured souls' play well into the popular myth of the nature of genius, and of course they can make excellent movies too.

The relationship between psychological health and art making, indeed any form of creativity, is complex and contains both positive and negative aspects. In recent times, artists have worked with the sick or traumatised using art as a form of therapy. For example, it has been used to support children in recovery from the effects of war or natural disaster. In this context the expression of psychological stress through art making can have a healing effect. The process involves the capacity of created images to express difficult emotions and healing occurs through the process of acknowledgement and reflection, which may be almost impossible to bear outside of the supported environment of creative therapy.

It is interesting to consider whether artists and designers generally might also benefit from some therapeutic potential of creative work, at least to some degree.

The vast majority of artists are not, of course, tortured by the burden of their creativity; however, the nature of the desire to create can set very demanding personal challenges. Solutions in creative work are rarely obvious; this is the nature of the challenge after all, and so it is both easy and necessary to become preoccupied with tasks. There is often a high level of investment in terms of time and energy and at times the work can become an intense experience.

An artist moves work from its start to completion, taking the disparate parts, ideas and materials and somehow bringing them to an integrated and complete whole. This investment in time, attention, energy and emotion is a psychic process as well as an artistic one and this takes the artist through various stages. As artists, we know the excitement and pull of the initial phases of creative work and this may feel difficult, unresolved and full of half-seen possibilities. As the work progresses feelings change and if the work goes well, there is often great satisfaction in the successful completion of an individual piece of work or a project.

During the 20th century the influential writer and critic, Adrian Stokes, proposed that there was a strong link between this type of experience and that of personal growth[23]. The cycle of moving from fragments to the whole in art making was explored as the metaphor for a journey to psychological maturity and health. This view no longer fits with the complexities of life in our post-modern world, as now we are perhaps less likely to view wholeness as the ultimate aim of psychic health. In the present era we have a more fluid and accepting attitude to contradictions and tension, but the opportunity at least remains for artists to see aspects of identity, disposition and personal change reflected in their work.

The process of making art is simultaneously outward and inward looking; artists look out to a shared social and cultural experience and are usually creating images to place into this world, yet their work also has the potential to allow them to reflect on their individual nature. What is revealed includes artistic interests, personal skills and abilities on one level, but also much less tangible dimensions such as aspirations and emotion. The characteristic ways in which artists deal with success and failure will also find a place in this process. It is inevitable then, that art making presents at least the possibility for self-reflection and self-development.

Whilst everyone changes and grows over time, there are sometimes special opportunities that are open to us as we make visual art. When artists make physical objects, they are sometimes able to see certain qualities of themselves revealed or embodied in their work. Occasionally and perhaps with the help

---

23 Stokes, Reflections on the Nude.

of others, they will see qualities they don't expect. This is an idea used very directly in art therapy; it works because a patient can often intuitively show something in an image which they cannot reveal in words to a therapist. As artists we can also benefit from this possibility, if we choose. We can look to our visual work as a trace of our own complex individuality. Unlike a therapist's patient we may not be experiencing such difficulty, but similar opportunities are there. As we grow as artists, we find that our creative work bears the mark not just of what we have learned about art, but also of what we know of the world and how our experience has been shaped over the years. Our creative images are born from the fluctuating imaginative space which exists between the world and ourselves and so these images can be diffused with a mood, an attitude, a style or content which can always offer an oblique reflection of who we are as individuals. Occasionally this can give a very direct impression.

A great deal of contemporary fine art in our post-therapy age invites this approach. Many artists themselves are often as much a subject of the work as any other content, and as such they sometimes seem like raw materials to be transformed by their own processes. This can seem more strongly evident with some of the current art personalities that are part of the market-ing of contemporary art. But however we work, in contemporary experimental ways or in more traditional ways, we are still left with the fact that art products present personal and individual qualities.

The precedent is clearly shown in the work of many artists. For example Cindy Sherman, Judy Chicago, Piet Mondrian, Jackson Pollock stand as clear examples of how a highly indi-vidual approach can help shape rich and varied artwork, one which is both deeply personal and yet also speaks to us in a broad cultural sense. The enthusiasms, interests and personalities of artists such as these are well and truly embedded in their art making. This often seems to be part of the strong attraction art holds for younger artists when they themselves are changing so quickly. The years across the late teens and early twenties are when the forging of personal identity and interests reaches a key level of maturity. For so many, this is when a connection between the journey through visual creativity and a sense of personal development, can become particularly intense.

These opportunities are not limited to this period though, as they can be a feature of creative work at any time. I am cautious about suggesting that these experiences are always for the best, simply that they occur and it is up to us how we might use them. There is a world of difference between a big dark Rothko painting, which presents his spiritual exhaustion and pre-suicidal depression and a late Mondrian, with its little red and yellow squares dancing across the white picture surface, displaying an enthusiasm for jazz and his love of New York city in an abstract image. Creative work can definitely give the opportunity for self-reflection and so may help us change and develop as people when and if we can.

If self reflection is part of the dynamics of the the inward facing creative process, it is the communication from artist to audience which defines the external or outward facing aspects of creativity. Visual art offers a unique quality and quite distinct experience for a viewer, since unlike many other creative products, images can be seen in an instant. Visual art is different in that other art forms require experiences to be followed through; a play has to be watched, a book read and music listened to, but visual images are present in their totality in a moment of time. Considerable time and thought may have gone into their creation, but the final presentation of images can have a unique immediacy and the whole image is there to be taken in at a glance. The process of making visual work has the capacity to gather up ideas and qualities, but ultimately these various relationships settle into a presentational form; they become present as a singular image. A further unique feature is that although the encounter with an image can happen with such speed, as time passes the image persists and the complete experience remains for the viewer. This quality of images to be present for an audience raises particular challenges and opportunities for artists. Makers have to be very close to the processes that generate images, yet they must also imagine a certain distance to get a sense of how the work might be received by others when it is complete.

Communication only becomes a possibility if the artist's vision becomes accessible to others. The implications of this can never be far from us as we work. Potential communication resides in the theme, the content, the mood, the simplicity or the complexity of the image. As we work over a period of time, with sets of ideas and often across series of images, these different qualities settle in different ways into individual pieces, and somehow we need to gauge how effective the work is. If we can imagine ourselves as a viewer we can ask questions, such as is the work matching our intention and becoming successful? And perhaps, what new possibilities are revealed as the image evolves?

As Winnicott suggests, communicating new possibilities often requires the reconfiguring of older traditions, and playful combining that draws in cultural associations in intriguing ways is often a productive approach to this. For example, Andy Warhol put together ideas about celebrity and consumerism in single images, Cindy Sherman used playful ideas about identity and gender with invented film stills, and Kazimir Malevich worked with geometry, colour and ideas about symbolism and spirituality. The best visual art layers up meaning, tradition and experiences. The effect these layers present in an image often works at a fairly intuitive level. Suddenly the whole work is there before us and we respond. Further time can then be spent with the image and meaning can be 'unpacked', or interpreted, as it is experienced by the viewer. But what is it that happens to a viewer in the first intuitive moment of contact for our communication to work well? One way to consider this is through the notion of an 'aesthetic' response.

The root of the word is the Greek 'esthesia', meaning 'an ability to feel sensation'. Any image creates a physical sensation initially as our eyes are stimulated. However, the response to an image is clearly more than a physical sensation and our word 'aesthetics' has come to mean much more than this too. Aesthetics is a philosophical term relating to the experience of beauty and ugliness. As artists we discover these qualities in our own and others' work. We know that our own activity is often not as direct as the pursuit of the beautiful and if this is direct, it is rarely simple. A work of art, or part of it, may be concerned with a much wider range of thoughts and feelings and so aimed at creating complex responses; aesthetic response can include anything from the sublimely beautiful 'wow' sensation to a stomach churning 'ugh', with a vast spread of qualities in between. This is not merely a psychological or physical experience; it is best conceived as a complex total response which can engage us on

141

many levels, visual of course, but through this, emotional, intellectual and spiritual as well. Aesthetic experiences may present a strong sense of physicality, spatial dimensions which we relate to through scale, volume and surface, or they might be light and ethereal. Images can attract, repel, invite, intrigue, even seduce; in short the full range and complexity of human response can become present in the moment of encounter, in an instant.

Aesthetic experience is not confined to art alone; many aspects of human life have these qualities, including of course the experience of nature. Occasionally we might see a stunning deep red sunset with a wide sky full of incandescent clouds. We can be caught off guard and overwhelmed for a moment; a common physical reaction is a sharp intake of breath and then we look and wonder. These classic images of transcendance also cause us to experience our human scale, our place on the surface of the planet, and the sense of the moment can seem to intensify. Like such a sight, aesthetic experiences in art can be packed with meaning through a breadth of association, memory and sensation; as we give attention we become entwined with a created image and discover imaginative implications and possibilities.

During the initial moment of viewing, so many aspects of ourselves are present, but the aesthetic encounter with the work rises up to meet us like a new thing, a new experience and we may start to develop and change something of ourselves through this encounter. This is not a process like learning a new fact, it is more like realising that our imaginative relationship with the world is not fixed, but that it can continually grow and develop if we are open to these opportunities. Aesthetic experiences through art expand the imaginative space which frames our relationship to the world; it is the role of creative artists to enrich the possibilities within this space for others.

I will end with a final thought about the nature of aesthetics and the experiencing of art that I first heard many years ago. The idea has remained with me, important to my own philosophy for both teaching and making art.

The idea comes from a way that the word aesthetic appears in common use. In a hospital we might have an 'anaesthetic' to subdue us and make us sleep. Aesthetics do the opposite; aesthetic experience through art can wake us up, enlivening rather than deadening. As an artist I recognise this; artists do seek to enliven and to contribute to life, rarely to erode it, especially when the work they make is sometimes perceived as challenging or problematic and it begins to create a new way of seeing for others. I have found through experiencing art and also teaching others about art, that I am continually surprised by how the vision and creativity of others can contribute to the richness of my own experience.

It is a challenge to reflect on what may be at the very heart of creativity, to consider how and what is communicated, why new things are made, and why it is that so much of what we value as creative work can be so surprising, unexpected and delightful.

I believe that the answer to this rests on the fact that what we do as artists involves the possibility of an encounter with the not quite known, not quite realised and not quite experienced. Creativity is an activity which hovers continually on the threshold of possibility, and as such, involves the artist with the privilege of close contact with something of the mystery of 'being' and being alive. Communication through creative work regardless of

143

discipline is so often about articulating this relationship in some way. We are shown things and led through experiences which can have a profound effect. As an audience we can be challenged, enriched, energised and made to feel more alive. The creativity of others can lift us out of the humdrum aspects of our existence and help us to appreciate the potential of our own humanity more sharply.

For the creative artist this is also where the necessity of the work lies. We all have the capacity to be creative to varying degrees, but some seem to have a disposition which draws them more strongly to actively explore this. Whether this is from something inherited, or due to key formative experiences, or the result of sudden unexpected moments of inspiration, it is clear that for some this is a path they must follow. Just as the creative work of others inspires and enlivens an audience, for an artist the experience of their own creative work is fundamentally energising and artists are fed and nourished by this experience; it seems to answer a need. Talk with artists about their own work, their creative concerns and interests and it quickly becomes clear that they have a passion for their work, and it is a passion which energises and animates them. It also makes them feel more alive as they explore the things that they are yet to know, and also the things they are yet to be.

Because of the relationship between time, culture and the continual potential of new work, artistic creativity is deeply paradoxical. It is absolutely fundamental both to human societies and individual experience, it is quite literally everywhere, and yet at the same time it is elusive and impossible to predict its effects. Almost by definition we cannot know quite how creative work will occur, nor do we know what the results will be,

144

although we have the knowledge that it does occur. We also have the faith that through our work we can be successful in playing a part in this exciting process, by which at its very best a greater and more fulfilled life can be built.

I hope that some of these thoughts will give encouragement, and perhaps offer some useful ideas for engaging with the immense challenge and opportunity that creative work in the visual arts presents. Above all, artistic creativity does not stand still and these ideas are really only some reflections on how to begin.

Review the work you have made over a period of time, choose years rather than months. Try to identify the individual pieces of work when you moved forward in a significant way, a time that was a high point, or a turning point, for you. What was the nature of this experience, what changed? Skill? Confidence? Style? Understanding? Be as particular and as specific as you can in this review.

If you were to write your artistic autobiography right now what would the significant chapter headings be? What is the story of the journey through your personal creativity so far?

Now look forward.
How would you like your art to develop?
What are the qualities you want in your art?
If there was one thing you could change about your work, or the way you work, what would it be?
What is the thing you most fear hearing about your work. What is the implication of this question honestly answered?

Some final thoughts:

If ten is finished, what number are you on?

If you need to try something out, try one hundred variations, no repeats.

Nothing can be precious, if a part of an unfinished work seems the very best part, destroy it, or it may hold you back from completing the whole work.

There is no right way to proceed, but have faith that you will recognise progress.

Every single part of a work should have significance; no padding, no backgrounds.

Try a new approach, become a new artist; then take your troubles with you.

All art has a subject, colours and shapes are containers for experience.

See something through to the very end, either to success or disaster, and then take it further.

BIBLIOGRAPHY AND REFERENCES

ADORNO, THEODOR (1991). *The Culture Industry*. London: Routledge.

BACHELARD, GASTON (1988). *On Poetic Imagination and Reverie*. Dallas: Spring Publications.

BEUYS, JOSEPH (1979). *Transformer*. New York: film by John Halpern.

EHRENZWEIG, ANTON (1993). *The Hidden Order of Art*. London: Weidenfeld and Nicholson.

ELKINS, JAMES (1999). *What Painting is*. London: Routledge.

ELKINS, JAMES (2001). *Why Art Cannot be Taught*. Illinois: Unversity of Illinios Press.

ERICSSON et al (1993). *The Role of Deliberate Practice in the Acquisition of Expert Performance*, in Psychological Review. Vol 100, No 3, 363-406.

FISCHL, ERIC and SALTZ, JERRY (1986). *Sketchbook with Voices*. New York: Alfred Van der Marck Editions.

GREENHALGH, PAUL (2005). *The Modern Ideal, The Rise and Collapse of Idealism in the Visual Arts*. London: V&A Publications.

HARPUR, PATRICK (2002). *The Philosophers' Secret Fire, a History of the Imagination*. London: Penguin.

HILLMAN, JAMES (1991). *A Blue Fire*. New York: Harper Perennial.

HILLMAN, JAMES (1978). *Further Notes on Images*. Dallas: Spring Publications.

JARMAN, DEREK (1995). *Chroma*. London: Vintage.

JONES, TIM (1999). *Artist Teacher Course lecture notes*. London: National Society for Education in Art and Design.

JUNG, CARL (1968). *Alchemical Studies*. Collected Works. Vol. 13. London: Routledge and Kegan Paul.

JUNG, CARL (1982). *Dreams*. London: Routledge and Kegan Paul.

KEARNEY, RICHARD (1991). *Poetics of Imagining, From Husserl to Lyotard*. London: Routledge.

MALPAS, SIMON (2003). *Jean-François Lyotard*. London: Routledge.

McCOMB, LEONARD (1983). *Exhibition Catalogue*. London: Arts Council of Great Britain.

NEWMAN, BARNETT (1947). *The First Man Was an Artist*. New York: Tiger's Eye magazine, ed. Ruth and John Stephan.

RICHTER, GERHARD (1995). *The Daily Practice of Painting*. London: Thames and Hudson.

SCHOENBURG, ARNOLD (1975). *Style and Idea, Selected Writings of Arnold Schoenberg*. ed. Leonard Stein. London: Faber and Faber.

SCHRANK, ROGER (2011). *The Twelve Cognitive Processes that Underlie Learning*. RogerSchank.com (accessed 23/7/11).

STOKES, ADRIAN (1978). *Colour and Form, The Critical Writings of Adrian Stokes*. London: Thames and Hudson.

STOKES, ADRIAN (1967). *Reflections on the Nude*. London: Tavistock Publications.

WINNICOTT, DONALD (1993). *Playing and Reality*. London: Routledge.

www.ingramcontent.com/pod-product-compliance
Lightning Source LLC
Chambersburg PA
CBHW070423290526
45791CB00005B/1815